TESTIMONIALS

I have been in the world of coaching for 30 years and been a professional coach since 1999. Over the years, I have spoken with many peers about their approach. Some have impressed, many have not. Max clearly falls into the first category. Recently, I have had the opportunity to share many conversations about coaching with Max. His passion for his craft is up there with the very best. He speaks in very ethical terms about his clients and places their well-being at the centre of his work. I have no doubt he will help many people live far more fulfilling and successful lives. The possibilities are limitless for Max and his clients.

Chris Chittenden
Ontological Theorist & Director - Talking About Pty Ltd

Max has the extraordinary ability to challenge you, to uncover the layers that subconsciously hinder your development, and then work with you to overcome them. He is dedicated to his clients and goes the extra mile every time. His preparation and ability to recall details said even a year ago help in making every session insightful while working towards long-term objectives. I can wholly recommend Max as a coach for anyone wanting to advance in business and their personal development.

Dr. Mark van Rijmenam
The World's #1 Futurist

Max's coaching throughout the year has proven remarkable results through my personal experience and significant outcomes were achieved. Max, a big thank you for your support and commitment in moving me towards my utmost potential. Without a doubt, I will continue to work with you on an ongoing basis and I look forward to our next session.

Domenic Morello
Co Founder & Partner - Nationwide Capital

I have been fortunate to know Max for a few years now, as he has evolved on his coaching journey. I believe one of the biggest compliments that one can be paid is when someone says, "You're doing the work you're meant to be doing". Well, I believe this to be true for Max. To be a great coach, you need to quickly gain people's trust, demonstrate authentic empathy and be able to hold a space for your counterpart to do the work they need to do. Max has these qualities in abundance. He is a passionate advocate for living a values led life and he truly believes in the possibilities that exist not just for some of us, but all of us. Max is already very good at what he does. He holds himself to the highest of standards and he expects this of his clients. As such, I have no hesitation in recommending him to anyone who is looking for that right person to coach, guide and support them in fully unleashing their potential.

Mike Read
Founder & Director - Pigs Can Fly Too

We have had the pleasure of working with Max for the past 18 months. During this time we made some bold family decisions, like to home school our children, continue to grow and contribute to two growing companies remotely, move to Manly Beach, Sydney, and expand our accommodation company, which our daughters have had full immersion in from the onset. We encourage a business and entrepreneurial mindset, a customized process of learning business and relish in the abundance of questions of what they individually show interest to. It's been a beautiful experience and quite daunting at times; it's been a process of elimination for what feels right for the family and what we are about and seeking moving forward. It has been a pleasure to share this with Max in parallel to his coaching practice. One of our family values at the forefront is having deep meaningful relationships and the opportunity of time, conversations, and many questions.

This is something we have come to experience with Max and respect and admire. We always look forward to a mutual relationship where we all grow and contribute to one another.

We are firm believers that the right people turn up at the right times. A quote within the family and our business at the moment is, "When the student is ready the teacher appears." Max has an innate ability to ask great questions and gives firm honest opinions also. An attribute that we admire and respect very much. Max needs to be on your team. It has been an awesome experience that is only just scratching the surface!

Ben Tindall
Founding Director - Follo & Villager Property

It's not often you come across someone who has found their calling in life. Max is one of these people. He possesses a sense of curiosity, warmth and discernment that makes others feel at ease and allows him to unlock their potential. I would have absolutely no hesitation in recommending Max to anyone wanting to improve all aspects of their life.

Bradley Chan
Chief Executive Officer - Banna Property Group

Working with Max to uncover the deeper layers of my behavioural patterns and personal narratives has been a profoundly rewarding and transformative experience, full of unexpected insights that have informed many other aspects of my life. His professional approach and methods for personal inquiry and self-development are predicated upon trust, honesty, and the courage to reinterpret what is possible for who you wish to become. Max is both supportive and accountable in tailoring a program to your own specific needs, and I'll be forever grateful for the breakthroughs we have achieved in our sessions. I encourage anyone wishing to unlock their fullest potential to consider working with Max as an invaluable part of that process.

Mark Coles Smith
Actor - Apple Cider Vinegar, Last Cab To Darwin, Modern Family, Mystery Road, etc.

Max has a preternatural balance of intelligence and heart. He listens carefully and prepares a program tailored to your goals and quirks. He studies your words, phrases, choices of response and finds references and language that is tailored exactly to effect growth and change.

Michael Rymer
Film Maker - Battlestar Gallactica,
Hannibal, American Horror Story, etc.

Working with Max has been inspirational. Max has helped me tackle specific issues or challenges in my life, and take steps towards improving them. Even in areas of my life where I thought there was nothing that could be done, he's helped me see that it's all down to mindset and beliefs. Max has great communication skills, and he asks the right questions at the right time. He has helped me verbalize my desires and goals, and form a tactical plan to move forward. I trust Max and feel comfortable telling him about my worries and the things that are holding me back. He is very supportive and non-judgmental and has helped me form a clear vision of what I want, and how to prioritize, so I can build the life I desire. I'd highly recommend working with Max to anyone ready for self-insight and self-development.

Laura Graham
Managing Director - Earthing Oz

Max I would like to give testimony to the series of Ontological coaching sessions you led with me. They have been deeply insightful and highly effective. The introductory format and written summaries are highly structured and illuminating, helping to crystallize concrete solutions to the specific issue we discussed. I plan to continue with them and will be recommending your service to several of my portfolio company founders.

Chris Barter
Co-Founder & Partner - King River Capital

I've known and worked with Max for many years. I've deeply appreciated his consistency and tailored support of my family. He has a great natural sense of reading people's mind and seeing what's behind the conversation between us and him. He has the strength of capturing the small details that might affect largely to the issues, as well as getting down to the central point of problems straight away, which makes his coaching very effective and efficient. He has supported both me and my sons in our development and always makes himself available to us whenever we have needed. I'm very grateful for all of Max's coaching and see myself working with him indefinitely.

Henry He
Chief Executive Officer - Medigate Medical Supplies

Working with Max has been nothing short of transformative. When I first engaged him, I was at a crossroads: ready to leave a long career in recruitment but unsure of what came next. Max helped me to clarify where I wanted (in fact, needed) to be, in a completely different space: the wine industry. What started as a fanciful idea to open a cellar door eventually evolved – through Max's guidance – into launching my own wine distribution business. Thanks to Max's sharp insight and encouragement, I not only launched this second business but did so having left other unviable options in the dust behind me. Those losses were mitigated before I'd even taken a step in the wrong direction. Max also connected me with invaluable contacts in the industry – some of whom I'm still working with today. Finally, on a personal level, Max stood by me through one of the most difficult chapters of my life. He helped me to navigate intense relationship issues and a near mental breakdown, always maintaining a balance of warmth, empathy, and professionalism. Max has been more than a coach – he's been a lifeline through both professional reinvention and personal upheaval. I can't recommend him highly enough.

Sabrina Maddock
Chief Executive Officer - Avanti Search

WHAT THE F*CK
**DO YOU
ACTUALLY
WANT?**

WHAT THE F*CK DO YOU ACTUALLY WANT?

FINDING A LIFE WITH PURPOSE

MAX STEPHENS

First published in 2025 by Dean Publishing
PO Box 119
Mt. Macedon, Victoria, 3441
Australia
deanpublishing.com

Copyright © Max Stephens

All rights reserved. No part of this publication may be reproduced, stored in a retrieval system or transmitted in any way or by any means, electronic, mechanical, photocopying, recording or otherwise, without the prior written permission of the author and publisher.

Cataloguing-in-Publication Data
National Library of Australia

Title: What The F*ck Do You Actually Want?
ISBN: 978-0-6489386-4-4
Category: Self-help/Personal Growth/Success

This publication is meant as a source of personal philosophical reflection and inspiration for the reader, however, it is not meant as a substitute for direct professional assistance or advice in regards to professional business matters or personal decisions.

The material reflects the author's personal experiences and opinions only and does not necessarily represent others' opinions or organizations the author has worked with. It is advised that readers should obtain appropriate independent professional advice concerning their own business or personal decisions.

Some stories have been recreated from the author's memory and some names and identifying aspects of individuals have been changed for privacy reasons.

The publisher and the author assume no responsibility for errors, inaccuracies, omissions, or any other inconsistencies herein and hereby disclaim any liability to any party for any loss, damage, or disruption caused by errors or omissions, whether such errors or omissions result from negligence, accident, or any other cause.

CONTENTS

Testimonials ~ i
Author's Note ~ xv
Introduction ~ xvii

Chapter 1 ~ 1
What the Hell Is Going On?

Chapter 2 ~ 21
How Do I Get Out?

Chapter 3 ~ 39
What Do I Do First?

Chapter 4 ~ 57
Why Do I Even Need a Purpose Beyond the Self?

Chapter 5 ~ 77
What's in It for Me?

Chapter 6 ~ 97
Calling Me a Hero Is a Bit Much, Isn't It?

Closing Words ~ 115
Appendix ~ 117
About the Author ~ 161

AUTHOR'S NOTE

FULL DISCLOSURE: I FUCKING hate self-help books.

They're usually filled with fluff, recycled ideas, and authors indulging in their own self-proclaimed genius. **Don't worry, you won't find that here.**

Originally, this book was over 80,000 words and 500 pages long. And then I realized that I was making the same mistake as every other self-help book. Adding too much. Overexplaining. Talking shit, basically.

So, I stripped it down. Every word in this book exists for one reason only: **to help you.**

And one of the ways I'll be helping you is through discussing some of the experiences I've had with my own clients. That's what I do: I work with people who are trying to sort their lives out, just like you. (Before the privacy police get all up in arms, I have indeed changed names, tweaked details, and in some cases, blended multiple client experiences into one story.)

So, throughout this book, you'll meet people like **Vanessa**, a high-flying executive who had everything on paper but couldn't shake the feeling that something was missing. You'll meet **Alex**, a young university student caught between what he truly wanted and what he thought he was supposed to want.

And then there's **Danny.**

Danny is different. His story doesn't fit neatly into the arc of transformation like the others. **Because Danny didn't change.** His story is, without a doubt, **the worst outcome of my career.** And that's exactly why he's in this book.

I don't think it's a mind-blowing announcement that most people don't change—not because they can't, but because they refuse to. **Danny is a reminder of what happens when you stay stuck.** I could've left his story out, but that would have been dishonest. This book isn't here to sell you some grandiose, utopian fantasy.

It's here to offer you the plain and simple reality.

So here it is. The distilled version. **No fluff, no filler, no wasted words—just exactly what you need.**

Now let's get to it.

INTRODUCTION

ALL RIGHT, LET'S GET something straight so we can kick off our journey together on the right foot.

Chances are, if you picked up this book, you have some kind of a problem in your life that you're looking to solve. You're looking for an answer, and you're open to finding one—but here in this book? Let's be honest with each other: You've got your doubts. And why wouldn't you? The personal development space is full of superficial advice and empty promises. You don't need more fluff, and you definitely don't need to be told what to do by someone who doesn't know the first thing about you or your life.

But consider this: Whatever brought you here isn't just about you. Western culture is in the grip of a crisis of meaning, and whether you realize it or not, you're caught in the middle of it. We live in a time of unparalleled material abundance, surrounded by comforts and conveniences that previous generations could only dream of. And yet, in spite of it all, we are the most disconnected, dissatisfied, and unhappy we've ever been. How is it that, in the most decadent period in human history, so many of us feel like something crucial is missing?

This book makes an unapologetic case that there absolutely is an answer to this "missing" feeling. But that answer isn't to be found in more success or more consumption. Nor does the solution lie in discipline or hard work—those are tools, not answers. The real solution lies in reconnecting with a deeper part of your intrinsic nature, one that modern culture not only neglects but actively works to suppress. The real answer involves not adding more to your life, but instead uncovering something more meaningful that's already there within you—something that actually has the power to redefine how you live.

This book calls it *A Purpose Beyond the Self.*

But before you roll your eyes or assume you've heard it all before, let me stop you, for this might not mean what you think. It's not charity, self-sacrifice, new-age nonsense, or a fleeting moral bandage to soothe your conscience. It's not about returning to outdated philosophies or comforting traditional narratives.

What will be presented to you is an invitation grounded in rigorous insights from psychology, neuroscience, anthropology, and sociology. But it only works if you do. In that sense, there's an implicit deal you're making by choosing to read this book: You have to take part actively. This isn't something you can skim through on a beach and then casually mention later, saying, "Oh yeah, I've read that book." That will not do.

But if you're willing to participate fully, the synergy between you and the book will provide you with answers. It may even give you the answer to the very problem that brought you here.

YOUR ROADMAP

Here's how this book is structured:

Each chapter begins with a **wake-up call**, a jolt designed to snap you out of autopilot and force you to question the comfortable narratives holding you back. While these sections may be challenging, they are not here to criticize; they're here to grab your attention and focus it where it matters.

Next, we move into a **deeper exploration** of the chapter's themes. This section lays the groundwork, connecting the dots to help you understand the bigger picture. Don't worry, these aren't dry, academic explanations; instead, they're designed to help you see in a clear and simple way why things are the way they are.

Next, you'll follow the journeys of **three central clients**. These are true stories that help bring the chapter's themes to life, showing how real people, each at different stages of development, have faced the same kinds of struggles you may be experiencing. As you read, see if you recognize yourself in any of them.

Following this, each chapter ends with **practical exercises**, designed to help you connect the ideas of each chapter to your individual life. So, take the time to complete them, as this is where the solutions to your problems will truly begin to take shape. Don't skip them.

Finally, every chapter will close with **the tough truths**, the rather **uncomfortable insights** that will challenge the way you think and drive the key points of every chapter home. If you're serious about resolving your problem, you'll need to face these truths head-on and reflect on them deeply before moving to the next chapter.

Oh, and one more thing: If you find yourself wondering, *Is there any actual research behind this?* flip to the **Appendix**. It's packed with studies and insights that will really help ground your understanding in facts and science.

WHO THIS BOOK IS FOR

So, who is this book for?

First, it's for **the high performers.** You've done everything you were supposed to: worked hard, climbed the ladder, checked all the boxes. But that rumbling of disquiet hasn't gone away. You're left wondering, *"Is this really it?"* If that sounds familiar, this book is for you.

Second, it's for **the ones just starting out.** Maybe you're stepping into the world and feeling the weight of endless options. Too many paths, not enough clarity. You want something meaningful, but you're afraid of wasting years chasing the wrong thing. If that's where you are, this book will help you discover what actually matters to you.

And finally, it's for **anyone who feels stuck.** Maybe life just hasn't worked out the way you hoped. You feel caught between indecision and self-doubt; or maybe you simply don't know how to move forward. Don't feel bad if you fall into this category: That's actually most of us, most of the time, on some level. This book is here to meet you where you are and help you find your way through.

A FINAL WORD

Yes, this book is here to guide you, but the path is yours to walk. Every page, every chapter, will reveal itself differently with each step you take. So, if you're willing to approach it as a part of your own journey, then let this introduction be the first step.

With that in mind, let's begin.
Good luck.

1
WHAT THE HELL IS GOING ON?

WAKE-UP CALL

LET'S NOT MINCE WORDS: You are in serious danger of screwing up your life. Not because you are lazy or unmotivated, but because the path you are on, whether you realize it or not, is a trap.

Maybe you've already built a life that others envy, or maybe you're still trying to figure it all out. Either way, chances are you're stuck on a treadmill leading nowhere meaningful: chasing goals shaped by somebody else, running harder and harder with no finish line in sight. If you do not stop and take a hard look at what you're doing, you will wake up one day filled with confusion and resentment, asking yourself, *How did my life end up like this?*

Have you ever wondered why you struggle with motivation? Don't be too quick to deny it, for the truth is, we all grapple with this issue in one way or another. But here's the thing: Your motivation suffers not because you need a good pep talk, or because you're "just a procrastinator," or even because of mental health issues. The reality is that your entire motivational system has been warped. Western culture has conditioned you to believe that fulfillment lies in an endless pursuit of more. The result is a growing disconnection from your fellow human beings, from your true motivations, from your intuition, and, most profoundly, from yourself. This system was not built to nurture you; it was built to sustain itself. It survives and thrives by keeping you dissatisfied.

The point is this: You can waste your life chasing the wrong things. You can piss away your potential, your energy, and your time chasing someone else's version of success. People do it every single day. I've seen it. And on some level, you know you've seen it too. If you do not stop now and ask yourself the hard questions, you risk living a life that will never really be yours.

The stakes are high, without a doubt.

But here's the truth: There is far more to you than you realize. You are capable of so much more than what you have been conditioned to believe. And yes, this book promises to be your no-nonsense guide to finding a life with purpose. But before we start that journey, there's a big question we need to confront:

How the fuck did we come to this?

A DEEPER EXPLORATION

To understand how you arrived at this moment, we need to step back in time. We need to uncover the roots of this narrative, to trace the historical origins that have reshaped not only society but the very way we define ourselves. Only by connecting these dots can we begin to understand the forces that shape the culture we find ourselves in today.

So, let's go back—to the fields, to the forges, to the dawn of industry, where the story begins.

Life once followed the steady rhythms of the land, the sun, and the seasons. Early morning mist lingered over rolling hills as farmers stepped onto damp fields, their hands roughened by years of turning the soil. This work was more than survival; it was a bond between the people and the earth they trusted to provide. In the village, the soft glow of a baker's oven broke the predawn darkness, filling the air with the comforting smell of fresh bread. The ring of a blacksmith's hammer echoed across the armory as tools and horseshoes took shape, each spark a reminder of the craft that built the community.

Every tool and every loaf carried the mark of its maker. A farmer's plow showed the wear of seasons past. A baker's bread was shaped by hands practiced in the art of sustenance. A blacksmith's tools were made to last, forged to serve the needs of the village. Work was not just something to get through; it was an expression of expertise and mastery.

The land was alive, a partner in the daily work of living. Streams cut through fields, feeding crops and quenching thirsty cattle. Forests offered timber for homes and shade for resting. The seasons guided life's pace: Spring brought planting, summer demanded long hours of labor, autumn delivered the harvest, and winter offered stillness and reflection. Each cycle tied people to the natural world and to each other.

Here, meaning itself was a lived experience. It arose naturally from the connection to the land, the rhythm of the seasons, and the shared work of the village. The meaning of life was the experience of living itself.

Then came the machines, shattering that natural rhythm. The Industrial Revolution didn't just bring steam engines and assembly lines; it rewired the human experience. Families left behind the fields and forges that had sustained them for generations, trading the open sky and familiar faces for the harsh glare of factory floors and the anonymity of urban living. Labor, once a source of pride and expression, became just another cog in the wheel of endless progress. The hum of the village gave way to the relentless grind of machinery, and the steady march of the seasons was replaced by the unyielding ticking of the clock and factory bells.

With this shift came an unintended consequence: a flood of goods that far exceeded what people truly needed. Assembly lines didn't just produce more, they redefined the meaning of "enough." With this surplus of goods came a new challenge: convincing people to buy more than what they really needed. And so began the rise of advertising, a new kind of storytelling. No longer were products sold for practicality alone; they were sold as symbols of aspiration. A house became a sign of success, a car a symbol of freedom. The seeds of consumer culture were sown, and with them, the narrative of "more" took root.

These ideals then became entangled with the American Dream—the alluring promise that anyone, regardless of their beginnings, could rise to the top through hard work and determination. For some, it delivered. For many, it did not, as systemic barriers like racism, sexism, and economic inequality ensured success remained elusive. Yet the narrative left no room for that truth. Failure, it suggested, was always personal.

The digital age accelerated this cycle into a frenzy, transforming how we live, connect, and measure our worth. Social media, once hailed as a tool for connection, became a breeding ground for comparison. Suddenly, your peers' lives weren't just nearby; they were in your pocket, filling your screen with curated snapshots of success, beauty, and perfection. The line between reality and performance blurred, as each post carefully crafted an idealized image, serving as a polished reminder of where you fell short. It wasn't about living a good life anymore; it was about *being seen* to live one.

This constant exposure reshaped how we define success, turning it into a public performance rather than a personal journey. The digital age galvanized an entire population with an insatiable drive to achieve, not for meaning, but for validation in a world that never stops watching.

And so, here you are, surrounded by abundance yet burdened by emptiness. That restless ache isn't failure; it's a calling, a quiet whisper meant for you, and you alone. Every day it whispers the same message to you of a truth long ignored:

This path is not the way . . .

So, the real question is not merely, "How did we get here?"

But instead . . .

Where do we go from here?

CLIENT STORIES

VANESSA:

I first met Vanessa in her office, a space that mirrored the precision in her demeanor. Perched in a high-rise overlooking the city, the room exuded authority. The walls were lined with sleek awards. Her tailored blazer, perfectly angled heels, and deliberate movements all spoke of control. Even her smile was calculated, more tool than expression of genuine warmth.

"They said you don't waste time," she said as she gestured for me to sit, her tone firm and efficient.

She had been referred to me by another CEO, someone I had worked with on a different challenge. Vanessa was 42, a senior partner at a top corporate law firm. She lived in a penthouse, drove a car that turned heads, and earned a seven-figure salary. On paper, she was unstoppable.

And yet, there was something off in her voice.

"I've been in a rut," she said, as if the words were foreign to her. "I need someone to hold me accountable."

The script was familiar. High achievers often come to me thinking they need a push. But they don't. It is almost never about pushing harder.

Her day was a blur of early mornings, client meetings, and late nights. Billable hours, high-pressure cases, squeezing more out of every hour.

As she laid out her grand plan, I interrupted. "What's the

most important thing in your life right now?" I asked, leaning in.

She hesitated, the mask cracking just a little. "Freedom and family," she said, but the hesitation lingered.

"Freedom from what?" I asked.

Her posture stiffened. "Look, I didn't come here for deep questions," she snapped. "I need practical help."

I let her words hang in the air, heavy with the denial of what she was really running from.

I listened further, letting her speak about the things that mattered—her family, the constant pressure to deliver—but her words felt hollow. Her son Oliver's soccer game came up. Vanessa had missed it, again. The guilt was thinly veiled in her steady voice. "He wouldn't talk to me for a full day after that," she admitted, the words quiet, almost inaudible.

Vanessa wasn't doing all this for her family. She was doing it to them.

Her husband, Mark, had stopped asking when she would be home. They spoke now only about logistics, the kids' schedules, and the household admin. "We're used to this," she said, her voice a little defensive.

Still, Vanessa was convinced she could fix it. "If I could just get back on track, everything would fall into place."

I paused, letting the silence fill the room. "You're deeply stressed. Your family is suffering, and you're clearly unhappy. And you're asking me to help you push harder?"

She leaned in, her voice sharp now. "Yes."

"You're a big one for directness, right?" I said. "Can I share what I see?"

Her gaze narrowed. "Go ahead."

I leaned forward slightly, letting the silence press in. "You're not successful. Not at all."

ALEX:

The first time I met **Alex**, it was over Zoom. He logged in promptly, adjusting his crisp black T-shirt and offering a warm smile that immediately struck me as genuine. Behind him, his university dorm room told a different story: an unmade bed, a few stray coffee cups, a half-eaten bowl of instant noodles, and a white-board covered with half-erased notes. For all his polished manners, the scene was a reminder that he was still just nineteen and figuring it all out.

Alex was the son of a long-time client of mine, and I had agreed to this meeting out of respect for his father. His dad, a kind, loving, and hyper-successful man, had come to me years ago after burning out from **building and leading one of the country's top tech companies.** The relentless pressure to perform at that level had taken a toll, not just on his health but on his relationships. His **wife had always valued financial security and success,** and as he began to step back from his career to reclaim his well-being, **the gap between their priorities only widened.**

At home, this divide became impossible to ignore. Many conversations around the dinner table turned tense, as discussions about Alex's future became **debates about ambition, risk, and security.** His father wanted him to find **meaning** in his work. His mother wanted to ensure **he never had to struggle financially.** Alex, caught in the middle, felt the weight of two opposing legacies pressing down on him.

"Thanks for doing this," Alex said, his tone earnest and respectful.

"It's my pleasure, Alex. It's nice to meet you."

From the moment he spoke, I could tell he was no stranger to performance. He had the polished tone and crisp delivery of someone used to impressing people, but there was something rehearsed about it, as though he had said these words many times before.

"How's life working for you, Alex?" I asked.

Alex was two years into a **business and economics degree**, earning top marks while plotting his entry into the corporate world. For the most part, he came off as a typical 19-year-old, balancing ambition with the kind of uncertainty that often accompanies big decisions at that age. He joked about pulling all-nighters, described his love of body surfing, and talked about wanting to travel "someday, when there's time."

"My dad worked so hard to give me opportunities," Alex said. "I feel like I owe it to him to make the most of them."

That line stayed with me.

"What drives you?" I asked gently. "What's meaningful to you?"

He hesitated, glancing at the books piled behind him. "Money, I guess," he said finally. "I want to make my parents proud. I want to build a life where I don't have to worry."

His sincerity was striking. But so was the shadow of fear.

I asked him, "And in a world where money was no object?"

"But it clearly is an object," he responded.

"That's true," I said.

He sat back, detecting insistence in my questioning. "I know I want to help people. I'm very interested in people," he said after a pause. "Helping people feels meaningful. But let's be real, emotional intelligence doesn't exactly pay the bills, does it?"

There it was—the tension between his heart and his head. Alex wasn't dismissive of his dreams; he was afraid of them.

"You know," I said, "your dad didn't come to me because he wasn't successful. He came to me because the success he had built didn't feel meaningful anymore."

Alex looked down, nodding his head, his expression thoughtful. "Sometimes when I'm at university parties, I go outside by myself and wonder if I'm chasing something that doesn't even feel like mine."

The honesty in his voice was rare, especially for someone his age—a testament to the exact emotional intelligence he was trying to dismiss. It was clear no one had asked him these kinds of questions before, and more importantly, he hadn't asked himself.

"What's stopping you from exploring something that feels meaningful to you?" I asked.

"Risk," he said simply. "What if I spend years chasing something that doesn't work out?"

"What if you spend years chasing something that doesn't matter to you?" I countered.

He didn't answer right away. Instead, he stared at the whiteboard behind him, the scribbled business strategies and career plans suddenly looking less certain. "I guess I've been so focused on getting ahead," he said finally, "that I forgot to think about where I'm going."

What really struck me about Alex was that, beneath his fears and doubts, there was a humility and openness that made him unique. It was a shame he didn't realize just how valuable those qualities really are in people. He wasn't stubborn because he refused to listen; he was stubborn because he cared too much about doing things "the right way."

As the session was coming to a close, Alex leaned forward. "Is there . . . any chance you'd do this again? I mean, meet with me?"

"I'll make you a deal," I said. "We can meet again, but only if you agree to one thing."

He raised an eyebrow, intrigued. "What's that?"

"Don't lie to me," I said.

Alex frowned slightly, his expression caught between defensiveness and curiosity. "I don't think I've been lying."

"Not on purpose," I said. "But I can feel it when it's not you talking. For someone as bright and emotionally intelligent as you, my bet is that you can too. From here on, you will speak with your voice."

He nodded slowly. "Okay," he said, his voice quieter now. "Deal."

The call ended, leaving me staring at the blank screen. Alex wasn't ready to rewrite his story, not yet. But for the first time, he sensed that the one he was living might not be his.

DANNY:

His name was Daniel, but everyone called him Danny. Even

on official paperwork, it was always just Danny. He liked it that way. Less formal, less bullshit.

The first time I met him, it was at his **auto repair shop**. He walked in a minute late, his work shirt smeared with grease, his handshake firm. The heat from the garage still clung to him, and his eyes were tired, but his movements were efficient. He was the type of leader who did it all himself. But I could feel the stress radiating from him.

He handed me a coffee. "Not bad, right?" he said, nodding toward the cup. **His accent was unmistakably English, working-class, direct, the kind that made everything sound like a statement.** "We don't do shit coffee here. Same as the work. If we're gonna do it, we do it properly." His hands were steady as he talked about the shop. The repairs, the customers, the reputation. His passion was clear, but so was the exhaustion underneath it.

He sat down across from me, wiping sweat from his forehead. "The team isn't selling enough high-ticket work," he said. "Customers come in for an oil change, and we aren't upselling them enough, that's the truth."

Danny had come to me for business coaching, but there was more to it. The market had shifted, squeezing his margins. The numbers were still good, better than most. But to Danny, they weren't enough.

"We used to have 40 percent margins," he said, frustration clear in his voice. "Now we're at 20, maybe 25 on a good month. It's not bad, but it's not what it was."

I pointed out that many businesses would envy those numbers. He shook his head. "It's not about the numbers. It's about what they mean. Where we should be."

I asked about his team. Danny's expression hardened. "I've given them everything," he said. "Salaries, bonuses, training. But they're just not getting it done. They're good lads, but they don't push. They wait for the customer to ask instead of telling them what needs doing. I don't get it. We could be making so much more if they just had some backbone."

I let that sit for a moment. "Or maybe," I said, "they know the difference between what the customer actually needs and what you're pushing them to sell."

His jaw tensed slightly. "That's bollocks. Every shop does it. It's not lying, it's about keeping the business alive."

There it was. The **real problem** wasn't the team's sales skills. It was **Danny's growing obsession with the business's success**, the pressure to **keep margins up at any cost.**

I asked what he ultimately wanted for his business. He softened. "I want to beat out the competition," he said, his voice steady but emotional. "Other garages have been doing this for generations. But I grew up watching my dad and uncles build this from nothing. I want to prove we belong with the big boys."

Pride, roots, determination. Danny wasn't just in it to win. He was in it to **honor where he came from.** But the weight of carrying that all on his own was starting to break him.

As I left that day, Danny's words stuck with me. This wasn't a man who didn't care about his work. His passion for the trade was clear. But somewhere along the way, the pressure—the market, the business, his own expectations—had knocked him off-kilter.

"**It is what it is**," he sighed, and the words stayed with me. They weren't just frustration. They were the quiet surrender of someone who had once been driven by a vision but had lost sight of it beneath the web of expectations and pressure.

PRACTICAL EXERCISES

SEEING BEYOND APPEARANCES—PART 1

1. **Find a fancy office building**
   Find a prestigious office building, a corporate headquarters, or a place that represents the kind of success you've been conditioned to chase. Look for places where high-level professionals work.
2. **Get yourself a coffee or sit nearby**
   Grab a nice coffee for yourself and find a spot in the lobby or nearby where you can observe without being noticed. Get settled, like you're sinking into a seat at the movies.
3. **Observe the people coming and going**
   Watch the people entering and leaving: the executives, the professionals, the ones who seem to have "made it."
   - Do they seem connected with life or distracted?
   - Pay attention to their faces. Do they look satisfied or stressed?
   - Listen to their conversations. Do they sound engaged and inspired, or is it all small talk and routine?

4. Question the appearance

Ask yourself:
- What are they truly seeking?
- What do their lives feel like on the inside?
- Is this success what they truly wanted, or simply what society conditioned them to want?

5. Reflect on your own busy-ness

If you're thinking, "I don't have time for this exercise" or "I'm too busy," stop. Notice that too.
- Are you so caught up in the hustle that you can't spare a moment to observe?
- What does that say about your own path?

6. Write down your reflections

Take a moment to jot down:
- What did you observe about the people around you?
- What was your initial reaction to seeing them?
- Do they seem fulfilled or worn out?
- How can you see yourself in them?
- Is this the life you want to live?

SEEING BEYOND APPEARANCES—PART 2

1. Find the most successful person you know

Identify someone who represents the kind of success you've been conditioned to chase—perhaps a boss, mentor, or family member. Choose someone who is widely seen as "successful."

2. Ask for a brief interview

Reach out and ask if you can speak with them for 10–15

minutes. Be clear that you're curious about their experience with success, not looking for advice or help. Play to their ego—they'll love that shit.

3. **Ask them these three key questions:**
   - "What's the hardest thing about being successful?"
     Pay attention not just to the words, but to the underlying honesty in their response. Do they mention stress, sacrifice, or dissatisfaction? Notice their tone. Do they sound energized or weary? Are they open about the challenges, or do they brush them off?
   - "Do you feel fulfilled by all of this?"
     This is the key question. The honesty in their answer is just as important as what they say. Do they answer with confidence, or is there hesitation? Is there an underlying sadness or emptiness that they might be avoiding? What is their body language telling you?
   - "Do you ever feel like something is missing?"
     Watch closely not just for what they say but for how they say it. Are they being truly honest with you, or are they just repeating what they think is expected? Does it look like they've ever asked themselves these questions? Pay attention to any shifts in their expression that might hint at the truth they're reluctant to share.

4. **Reflect on their answers**

   As they speak, notice:
   - Are they content, or does something feel off?
   - If you detected something is missing, what might that be?
   - Are they living their dream, or fulfilling expectations set by others?

- Does their success feel like a personal triumph, or is it a societal achievement they feel pressured to uphold?

5. Write down your reflections

After the interview, take a moment to jot down:
- What stood out to you in their answers?
- Did they seem content or unsure about their success?
- How does their perspective align with your view of success?

SO, WHAT'S THE POINT?

You now have both a high-level perspective from observing "the successful" as well as a first-person account of what you've been conditioned to pursue.

Now ask yourself honestly: *Does this really look like success to you?*

THE TOUGH TRUTHS

- **Your version of success is not yours.** It's a **cultural hand-me-down**, a script you inherited without questioning if it actually fits.
- **You are running on a treadmill with no finish line.** The faster you go, the further you get from a life that's actually yours.
- **You've been conditioned to want things that will never fulfill you.** And the system depends on your dissatisfaction.
- More money, more status, and more recognition will not fix the ache inside you. It will only distract you from it.
- You think you're making choices, but your choices have already

been made for you through your cultural narrative. The only question is whether you'll wake up to this.
- **The price of staying on this path is your life.** Not in the distant future, but right now.

20   What the F*ck Do You Actually Want?

2
HOW DO I GET OUT?

WAKE-UP CALL

LET'S NOT OVERCOMPLICATE THIS. You don't need a PhD in sociology or a stack of research papers to see what's going on. Sure, the appendix of this book is packed with studies, and they may make me seem clever—which I totally am—but the truth is, you don't even need them. All you really need to do is look around you. Look at your own life. Tell me. How's it working out?

Be honest. I don't want the surface-level answers you give at work or the polite ones you save for family dinners. I'm talking about the truth. Is there a part of you that wonders if all this running—this endless juggling of tasks, goals, and responsibilities—is actually getting you anywhere that matters?

Think about your days. The alarms that wake you before you're ready. The endless list of things to do. The way time feels like sand slipping through your fingers. You hit the pillow exhausted but unsatisfied, hoping that tomorrow will somehow feel different. Yet, today is yesterday's tomorrow. Does it feel any different?

Now think about what you're chasing. Is it the next promotion so the financial strain will ease its grip on your chest? A car to impress people that don't really care about you? Travel as a chance to briefly escape? Or maybe it's none of those things. Maybe it's just the idea of arriving at some future moment where all this striving will finally make sense. But here's the real question: Has that moment ever come? And if it hasn't, what makes you think it ever will?

Look closer. When was the last time you felt deeply content? Not distracted, not entertained, not briefly relieved, but truly at peace? When was the last time you looked at your life and thought, "Yes, this is exactly what I want"?

This isn't about judgment. You didn't create this problem, but you are living in it. We all are. The system is designed to keep you chasing; it's a treadmill that promises fulfillment is just one more step away. And when that step doesn't deliver, the system says, "Don't worry, that's just because you haven't made it there yet." Wherever the fuck "there" is. You see, the system isn't broken. It's working exactly as intended.

But here's the thing: You don't have to tolerate this shit.

No one's asking you to renounce modern life or join a protest. No one's telling you to quit your job or throw away your possessions. The answer to the question "What am I supposed to do?" doesn't start with dismantling the system. It starts with asking—and answering—the simplest question of all: *Is this working for me?*

Because here's the truth: It doesn't take grand gestures to change your life. It starts with seeing clearly—I mean really *seeing*—the patterns that keep you stuck. The way your choices are driven not by what you truly want, but by what you think you're supposed to want. The way you sacrifice your health, your relationships, even your well-being, for shallow rewards that never feel like enough.

Again, this isn't about fixing the world. It's about fixing how you live in it. It's about taking real ownership of your life and reclaiming the ability to make choices that are yours.

Take a moment. Look around. Look inward. Face it, once and for all.

Right here and now, make a commitment with me:

I will do something about this. I may not know what yet. But I know this must change.

A DEEPER EXPLORATION

In the first chapter, we began to unravel the cultural narrative that shapes the world around us. But there's a deeper layer beneath it, one that's far more personal and powerful: the nature of narrative itself. Stories are so fundamental to the human condition that they're mostly invisible, like water to a fish. They're the lens through which you see the world, the script that guides your decisions, and the meaning you attach to your life. They are so embedded in your experience that you rarely question them. But now, you're going to learn how to see through them. Read the following exploration closely. Challenge yourself to open your eyes.

A fire burns low in the heart of the village, its golden glow pulsing against the deep black of the night. The scent of woodsmoke mingles with the earthy aroma of dry soil, filling the crisp air. Shadows flicker across weathered faces, their lines briefly illuminated before fading back into the darkness. The soft murmur of voices rises and falls, blending with the crackle of the flames.

Among the people sitting around the fire, one figure is more striking than the rest, the chief. His skin, like the bark of an ancient tree, speaks of decades under sun and storm. His voice, deep and deliberate, carries above the flames, weaving stories of their people. His hands move as he speaks, tracing shapes in the air, stitching tales into the night. The firelight gleams in his eyes, reflecting seasons and the weight of shared history.

For our ancestors, stories were not about individual glory; they were sacred vessels of connection. Tales of the great hunt, the storm that tested endurance bound the group to one another, to the land beneath them, and to the stars above.

Stories passed wisdom from one generation to the next, revealing meaning and deepening a sense of belonging. They were prayers carried on smoke curling into the sky, rituals grounding the people in the eternal cycle of life. The elder's words, punctuated by the crackle of the fire, made the stories feel alive, as though the ancestors themselves were present, leaning in to listen. Stories were the bedrock of the human condition, the sacred art of being alive.

The problem is not stories. The problem is what has happened to them.

The firelight dimmed, replaced by the cold glow of screens. The shared stories that once connected us became fractured, and in their place arose a single, dominant narrative: *consume more, achieve more, be more*. Where stories once connected us, this current story isolates us. Where they once enriched our humanity, filling our hearts, this story convinces us we are not enough as we are.

Pause here for a moment. What you're about to read isn't just another critique of consumerism. It's a glimpse into the core mechanism of the trap. If you're willing to truly see it, and all its implications, the illusion begins to unravel. It's uncomfortable, but it's also liberating. Because once you see through it, you can't unsee it.

Let's take a Gucci scarf, for example. You don't buy fabric. You buy a story. You're not buying the scarf; you're buying the promise it whispers: elegance, sophistication, success. You're buying the belief that owning it enriches your own story, declaring you someone who has elegance, sophistication, and success. But here's the trick: As soon as next year's line is released, the Gucci scarf you currently own no longer signifies the same level of success. Actually, it says you're falling behind. And it's the same fucking scarf.

Isn't that absurd?

YOU NEVER BUY THE THING—YOU BUY THE STORY OF WHAT OWNING THE THING SAYS ABOUT YOU.

This is the game. You cannot go any further in this book until you grasp this. This is not an accident. It's not a flaw in the system. *It is the system.* The stories you chase are designed to expire, ensuring you remain in pursuit. The car that made you feel powerful when you first drove it becomes ordinary when a newer model appears. The promotion that felt like progress is overshadowed when someone else gets a bigger title. The house that once felt like success now just feels like the place you sleep.

Are you getting this? This is how it works! You are constantly distracted with the promise of "better", so you never pause to ask: Is this stupid game even worth playing? The stories tied to these symbols of status, wealth, and success are always shifting, always keeping you running. That's why we mentioned in Chapter One that you're on a treadmill—just because you're running, doesn't mean you're going anywhere.

Breaking free from the trap doesn't mean rejecting modern life. It doesn't mean you should throw away your Gucci scarf or renounce ambition. It means recognizing these stories are just stories, and stepping outside the whole game, as though awakening from a dream. And for the first time, you can finally ask yourself this question:

What kind of life do I really want?

And when you do, you don't just have the opportunity to rewrite your story. You have the chance to reclaim your life.

CLIENT STORIES

VANESSA:

A few months into working together, **Vanessa** had achieved what she came to me for: breathing space. Her calendar was no longer an unforgiving gauntlet. She had evenings free, mornings that started with coffee instead of chaos. By all accounts, we had done what she'd asked.

But as she sat across from me, overlooking the city skyline, something unspoken lingered in the air.

"You've got the space now," I said. "How does it feel?"

She hesitated, her eyes flicking to the window. "It's fine," she said, her tone flat. "I'm less stressed. That's good, I guess—right?"

"You guess?"

Her gaze snapped back to me, sharp. "What do you want me to say? I'm not overwhelmed anymore."

"It's what you said you wanted," I replied. "Does it feel like enough?"

She stiffened. "What kind of question is that?"

"An honest one," I said. "So, does this feel like enough?"

The room fell silent. Her fingers drummed lightly on the edge of the desk. "I'm not unhappy," she said finally, though it sounded more like a question than a truth.

"Okay," I said. "But what's all this for? The work, the late nights, the goals. What's the point of it all? The bigger point."

Her lips pressed into a thin line. "The point is to succeed. To win. Isn't that what people like me are supposed to do?"

"Is that what you think?" I asked. "Or is that what you've always been told?"

Her jaw tightened. "Look, I'm not here for some philosophical debate. I came to you to help me manage my time, and we did that. So why are you pushing this?"

"Because I don't think you're satisfied, Vanessa," I said quietly. "And I think you know it."

Her polished mask cracked slightly. Her fingers stilled, but her tone remained guarded. "I'm fine."

"Are you?" I asked, leaning forward. "Or have you just gotten better at dodging the truth?"

Her gaze faltered, a flicker of doubt breaking through. She looked away for a moment, her hands settling in her lap. "I don't know," she admitted, her voice quieter now.

"Have you ever stopped to ask yourself: Why am I doing any of this at all?"

The silence deepened. Her shoulders dropped slightly, and her gaze softened. Finally, she looked up, her voice hesitant but honest. "I guess I haven't. Not really."

"That's okay," I said gently.

The room felt different now. Her gaze wasn't hard or defensive anymore. It was cautious but open. Searching.

For a moment, she sat there, her eyes distant, as though piecing together something unfamiliar. Then, almost imperceptibly, she began to nod, the movement slow but deliberate.

Vanessa wasn't ready to leap, but she was beginning to see.

ALEX:

When I logged into our session, **Alex** was already there, leaning into the camera, his face tight with frustration. The polite smile from our first meeting was gone. Behind him, the usual chaos of his dorm room felt louder somehow: a coffee-stained mug, an empty energy drink can, and his whiteboard crammed with scrawled equations and ideas, many angrily crossed out.

"Okay," he said, skipping any greeting, his tone clipped.

"I've been going in circles all week, and it's killing me."

I nodded. "What's been on your mind?"

He sighed, dragging a hand through his hair. "I can't stop thinking about it. I'm lying awake at night, replaying the same questions: What if I'm wasting time? What if I'm doing the wrong degree? What if I screw up my entire future?"

His words spilled out in a rush, frustration building with every sentence.

"My dad was already working as an **engineer** at my age," he added, voice rising. "He was juggling a full-time job and university, pulling insane hours. Now look at him. He was so far ahead, and I'm stuck in this dorm, overthinking everything and going nowhere."

He exhaled sharply, his hands gripping the edges of his desk. "Every day I don't figure this out feels like another day wasted."

I let his words settle in the silence before leaning forward. "That sounds exhausting."

"It is," he snapped, then hesitated. "I mean . . . yeah. It is."

"You're very self-aware, Alex," I said. "Most people your age aren't wrestling with the internal conflict you are. That's a real strength."

He crossed his arms, his defenses snapping back into place. "Everyone says that. My family's always going on about how I'm good with people, how I'm emotionally intelligent or whatever. But honestly? It feels like a consolation prize. Like they're saying that because I'm not as intellectually strong as everyone else."

"Why is emotional intelligence a consolation prize?" I asked.

His jaw tightened. "What am I supposed to do with it? Be a therapist? No offense, Max, but I'm trying to make a lot more money than you."

I laughed. "None taken. But tell me this: If what your dad has achieved is so important to you, how do you achieve anywhere near that if you dismiss your strengths?"

He stared at me, his mouth tightening. Then he glanced at his whiteboard. "I probably won't," he admitted, voice quieter now. "But it doesn't feel like enough. Emotional intelligence feels . . . intangible."

I nodded. "Alex, you admire your dad, right? What does he think?"

He hesitated, his conflict written all over his face. "He says it's great. He's proud of me for being good with people. But . . . I don't know. It feels like he's just trying to make me feel better."

I leaned in slightly. "So if your dad and I are in agreement, have you ever considered that you might be the one who's wrong here?"

Alex didn't answer right away. Instead, he stared at the desk, his fingers tapping nervously.

"I really don't want to screw up," he said finally. "I just . . . I don't know."

"Can I share what I see?" I asked gently.

He nodded, wary but open.

"The only wrong move you're making is disowning who you are. You're not your dad, Alex. You don't have to be. But you'll never find your own path if you keep rejecting yourself."

He frowned, crossing his arms tighter. "So what do I do?"

"You want to get moving, right?" I asked.

"Yeah," he said cautiously.

"Well, let's start with who you are. Triple down on your strengths. Emotional intelligence has the potential to make you far more valuable to the market than you realize."

His jaw tightened, his resistance flaring again. "What if it doesn't work?"

I let the silence hang for a beat before answering.

"Alex, you're sitting here, driving yourself in circles, chasing a version of success that doesn't even feel like yours, trying to become someone you're not—does that sound like a better plan to you?"

He let out a sharp exhale, looking down at his desk. "I guess not," he muttered.

"I agree," I said firmly.

He leaned back, his arms still crossed, but his shoulders had eased. The tension was still there, but so was something else, a crack in the resistance. For the first time, Alex was starting to see that maybe, just maybe, there was a different path forward.

One that might actually be his.

DANNY:

When I arrived at **Danny's garage** to run the workshop, the place smelled of oil and warm rubber, the faint scent of petrol lingering in the air. But the atmosphere inside the office was anything but warm.

The team sat stiffly in the small break room, their polite smiles thin, their energy cautious. It was the kind of tension you could feel before anyone said a word.

"All right, lads," **Danny** said briskly, standing at the back with his arms crossed. "Maxie the Motivator here is going to get you back on track. Listen up. We need results."

The way he said it wasn't friendly—it was performative. A dig.

I started the session the same way I always do, **focusing on building trust** and creating a space where people felt safe to speak. Slowly, the team began to open up.

One mechanic shared how they struggled to **sell extra services without feeling like they were ripping people off**. Another admitted they **felt uncomfortable pushing unnecessary repairs**, even when Danny insisted that to do so would just be "good business sense."

The concerns were real, **understandable**—and a clear signal of something deeper.

Danny sat at the back, arms still crossed, **eyes narrowed slightly as he listened**.

"Come on," he interrupted, his voice sharp. "We've been over this already. Stop making excuses. If you can't handle it, maybe you're not cut out for sales. This is how the game works."

The room fell silent. Whatever openness had been building **vanished instantly**. One by one, the team withdrew, their words cautious, their energy deflated. Danny's frustration **hung heavy in the air**, his tone sharp enough to cut through the progress we had been making.

I guided the session back on track, **offering strategies for handling customer objections** while keeping integrity intact. Slowly, the team began to **re-engage**, but the initial spark of openness was gone. Their hesitation lingered, a clear **reflection of the tension in the room.**

By the end of the session, it was obvious there was **potential within the team,** but what was holding them back was becoming even clearer. **As the team filed out, avoiding eye contact with Danny, he stayed behind, leaning against the wall with his arms crossed.**

"So?" he asked, his tone flat. "What's the diagnosis, coach?"

The way he said it made it clear **he wasn't asking. He was challenging.**

I met his gaze. "I think your team **doesn't feel safe to sell the way you want them to."**

His frustration **boiled over.** He let out a harsh laugh and shook his head.

"But I've given them everything!" he snapped. "They've had training, bonuses, everything they need. They're adults—surely I don't need to babysit them as well!"

"Okay," I said. "Why do you think they're holding back?"

His jaw tightened. "Because they're soft," he said flatly. "And besides, I have a sales coach now, don't I? Maybe I should ask him," he added, **staring at me now, deliberate, almost smirking.**

Before I could respond, there was a knock at the door.

One of his **mechanics** stepped in, hesitating. They handed Danny a folded piece of paper.

"What's this?" he asked.

The mechanic **scratched the back of his neck** but didn't answer.

Danny froze, staring at the paper.

"You're quitting?"

PRACTICAL EXERCISES

PART 1: REVISITING THE STORIES OF YOUR ACHIEVEMENTS

1. **Choose Something Meaningful:**
   - Find an object you own that once felt like a big accomplishment (e.g., a graduation diploma, a promotion plaque, a designer item, or even a car). Alternatively, think about a significant achievement you've celebrated in the past.
   - Hold the item or think about that moment. Close your eyes for a second and try to recall how you felt at the time.
2. **Ask Yourself:**
   - How did this item or achievement make me feel when I first got it?
   - What story did I attach to it? What did it symbolize about who I was or what I had accomplished?
3. **Now, Look at It Today:**
   - How do you feel about it now?
   - Has the story you attached to it changed? What meaning does it hold for you today?
4. **Reflect and Write It Down:**
   - Was the item or achievement itself the source of your joy, or was it the story you told yourself about it?
   - Did the achievement deliver the fulfillment you expected, or has its meaning faded with time?

PART 2: QUESTIONING THE STORIES BEHIND YOUR GOALS

1. **List Your Goals:**
   - Write down your top five goals for the next year. These could be professional, personal, or material (e.g., a promotion, buying a house, taking a vacation, hitting a financial milestone).
2. **Ask Yourself:**

   For each goal, answer these questions:
   - What do I believe this goal will give me?
   - What story am I telling myself about this goal? (e.g., "If I achieve this, I'll be ____.")
   - Have I ever achieved something similar before? If so, did it fulfill me in the way I expected?
3. **Challenge the Promises:**
   - How do I know happiness, freedom, or fulfillment is waiting on the other side of this goal?
   - Am I chasing the goal because it's meaningful to me, or because I've been led to believe it's what I'm supposed to want?
4. **Reflect and Write It Down:**
   - What patterns do I notice in how I view my achievements and my goals?
   - Are my goals rooted in my own desires, or are they shaped by societal conditioning?

SO, WHAT'S THE POINT?

You have now seen through the game. You understand it now

from a historical and cultural perspective as well as directly in your individual life.

Finally, you can begin crafting a life that is yours.

Do not fall back asleep.

THE TOUGH TRUTHS

- You don't actually know what you want. You only know what you've been told to want.
- You tell yourself, "It'll all make sense once I get *there*." But how many times have you said that before?
- Your exhaustion isn't just physical, it's existential. Deep down, you know something is off, but it's easier to stay busy than to face it.
- If you don't take control of your life, someone else will. And chances are, they already have.
- You keep waiting for the moment when everything will finally "click" and life will feel complete. That moment is never coming, unless you create it.
- You never buy things. You buy what owning them says about you.

38   What the F*ck Do You Actually Want?

3
WHAT DO I DO FIRST?

WAKE-UP CALL

WELL DONE. YOU'VE AWAKENED from the dream. You've dismantled the illusions, broken free from the stories that weren't yours, and now you're standing on the other side of the fence. But here's the truth: Stepping out of the game is only half the battle.

So . . . now what?

Well, now comes the most important work of all: We begin to rebuild. Not the life you thought you wanted. Not the life others told you to chase. But a life that is undeniably, unapologetically your own. A life of meaning. A life that's worth waking up for every single day.

Leaving the game behind isn't the finish line. It's the starting point.

But before we go further, you need to make a crucial commitment: **Do not fall back asleep.**

The comfort of old habits and storylines will try to lure you back. The pull of the familiar will whisper that it's easier to return to chasing the old goals, to settle for the empty rewards you've just left behind. Don't listen. Don't let your hard work go to waste. You've come too far to lose yourself again.

You've had insights along the way. Big ones. Foundational ones. But they're just that: foundations. What lies ahead isn't just about living free from all those stories—it's about creating an incredible life anew. A life that feels whole, aligned, and deeply fulfilling. A life that isn't just the avoidance of pain but one that aspires something far greater. Why? Because you only get one.

So, how do we do this?

DEEPER EXPLORATION

The runway is in front of you, stretching wide and open. But it's not clear. Not yet. Years of accumulated baggage, distorted perceptions, and unresolved pain clutter the path. If you want to take off, if you truly want to answer the question found in the title of this book, the runway must be cleared.

This part of our journey is about three tools that will help you do that: **Radical Honesty, Forgiveness,** and **Mortality.** These aren't abstract concepts—they're practices, ways of seeing, and shifts in understanding that cut through the noise. They're not here to complicate your life; they're here to free you from the layers of intoxication, resentment, and illusion that keep you from living the life you want.

Radical Honesty is your way back to solid ground. You've spent years being told what to do, how to live, and what should matter. Layer upon layer of expectations and conditioning have clouded your sense of self, leaving you unsteady and unsure. At its core, radical honesty is about learning to discern truth for yourself.

So how do you tell the difference between truth and conditioning? You can *feel* the difference. Truth is solid and undeniable, like standing on firm ground. It doesn't need justifications, explanations, or arguments; it resonates deeply. Lies, no matter how subtle, feel fragile and uneasy. They rely on excuses, reasoning, and a constant need for validation. Most importantly, they make you feel weak. If you need to prop something up with "because," it's likely untrue. Truth doesn't beg to be believed; it simply exists.

Think back to a time when you were confronted with a truth

you couldn't deny. Maybe it was about your life, a relationship, or a decision you had to make. It might have been uncomfortable, even painful, but it was undeniable. How did you know? You felt it, deep in your body, as if your entire nervous system recognized it. That is the essence of truth. It doesn't just sit in your thoughts; it lands with weight, grounding you, even when it's painful.

Radical honesty isn't easy, but it's freeing. Strip away the conditioning, and you'll uncover what's real. It might feel like a cold splash of water, but in that clarity lies your foundation. Keep this close, because recognizing and trusting your truth is essential as we move forward.

Radical honesty reveals truths you've avoided—about others, about yourself, and about the weight you've been carrying. And this brings us to **Forgiveness**, the tool that ensures you truly close the last chapter behind you. You might think forgiveness doesn't apply to you, that there's no one you need to forgive. But don't make that mistake. Every one of us carries hidden weights: grudges, guilt, shame, and unresolved pain. These pain points are anchors that tether you to the past, quietly influencing your present and shaping your future.

Forgiveness isn't about excusing others or erasing the past. It's about reclaiming your energy and power. Resentment, guilt, and regret sap you of the strength you need to create a new path forward. To forgive is to set down the burdens you've unknowingly carried and release yourself from their grip. You may be surprised, as you reflect, by how much you've been holding onto—a grudge that still stings, regret over a missed chance, or shame for not measuring up. These weights sap your potential, keeping you tied to what was instead of what could be.

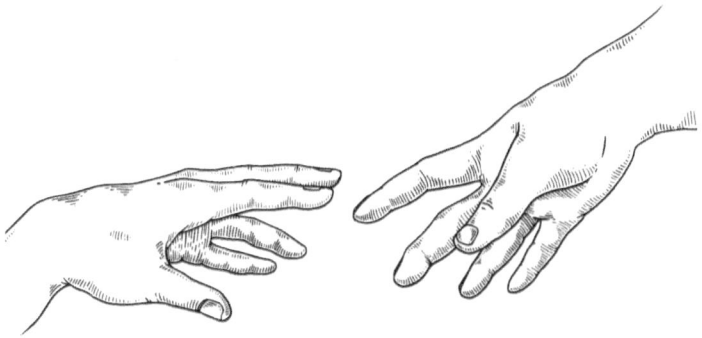

Forgiveness is an act of liberation. It's not for others; it's for you. It's how you ensure the past stays in the past, no longer following you into each step forward. Close this chapter of your life fully, and you'll discover a kind of freedom that creates space for something new. This is how you begin a new chapter—from a place of deep peace.

Once you've released the past, you can turn your full attention to the present. And this is where **Mortality** offers its gift. Mortality, the ultimate clarifier, is the one commonality that levels us all. When you truly grasp that your time is finite, the unimportant things lose their grip. The distractions, the fears, and the petty concerns dissolve, leaving only what truly matters. It strips away the illusions and brings you face to face with the raw truth of your priorities.

When you realize you're not getting out alive, you stop playing it safe. You stop waiting for "someday," because you understand that someday is a lie. Everything will crumble eventually, so why not take the leap now? Mortality is not a threat; it's a gift. It reminds you that your time is the most precious currency you have, and once it's spent, you can't get it back.

Let this realization sober you: You are absolutely, without a doubt, going to die. Let the finality of this insight sharpen your focus. Now that you're in touch with this, what will you stop doing? More importantly, what will you start doing?

Without the work of this chapter of the book, you'll remain trapped in self-delusion. With it, the path is clear, and you have a chance to rise higher than you ever thought possible.

Stop waiting for clarity. Stop waiting for permission. **Take action now.**

You'll figure it out as you go, but if you don't begin now, nothing will change. And you know it.

CLIENT STORIES

VANESSA:

When **Vanessa** arrived at her office building lobby for our next session, she looked more present than ever (no doubt the freed-up calendar was helping with that), but there was an edge to her calmness nonetheless. Her notebook landed on the table with a faint thud, and she sat down, letting out a short sigh as she ordered her coffee.

"You asked me to think about why I do what I do," she said, cutting straight to the point. "I wrote some things down.

What Do I Do First?

But I don't know if they're what you're looking for."

I leaned back. "Let's hear it."

She flipped open the notebook. "Family, my team, giving back. The usual suspects." Her voice was flat, dismissive. "I mean, it's fine, right? Those are good things."

"And how did it feel to write them down?"

She hesitated. "Fine, I guess."

I waited.

"They're . . . nice ideas," she added finally, but her words hung in the air like unfinished sentences.

"It sounds like there's something else," I said. "Something you didn't write down."

She froze, her hand stilling on the notebook's edge. "No," she said quickly. Then, after a pause, "Well . . ."

"What came up?"

"It's stupid."

"Tell me anyway."

She looked down at the notebook, her fingers tightening around its edges. "I thought about my grandmother," she said quietly.

I didn't respond, giving her the space to continue.

"She was incredible," **Vanessa** said after a moment. "Fearless. Full of life. She used to tell me stories about her childhood while we drank tea after school. I wanted to make her proud. Everything I've done—my career, my success—was for her, in a way."

Her voice wavered. "But in the end, she . . . changed. When she moved into a senior home, it was like all that life, all that fire, just disappeared. She wasn't mistreated, but it was like she'd stopped living before she even died."

She swallowed hard, her gaze distant. "I remember thinking: **This can't be how it ends. Not for her. Not for anyone."**

Silence fell between us, thick with the weight of her words.

"You know, I had this idea back then," she said finally. "What if there were places where people could really *live* their final years? Not just be cared for, but laugh again, connect, eat meals that made them feel alive."

Her voice softened. "What if there was something more? Like helping them let go of regrets, find forgiveness, find peace with themselves and others. So that when the time came, they could leave this world feeling whole. Loved. Like they mattered."

The vulnerability in her voice made the moment feel almost sacred. But then, as quickly as it had come, she shook her head. "But it's ridiculous," she said, her tone hardening. "I wouldn't even know where to start. It's not realistic."

"Wait," I insisted, ensuring her eyes met mine. "Why not?"

She blinked. "Because," she said sharply, "I don't know anything about that world. And I don't have time to think about it now. Anyway, I have a meeting to get to."

Vanessa stood abruptly, sliding the notebook into her bag. Her polished exterior returned, her voice steady. "Thanks for the session," she said, already turning toward the elevators.

I watched her go. Just as she was about to step inside, I called out, my voice quiet but deliberate.

"Every day you sit in your high-rise office chasing success, there are grandmothers just like yours, staring out the window, waiting to die."

She froze.

For a moment, she didn't turn around. Then, slowly, she glanced back at me, her eyes meeting mine, a tear slipping free before she turned and stepped into the elevator.

The doors closed.

Our session was over, for now.

ALEX:

Alex logged into our next session with a noticeable heaviness in his expression. His usual polite demeanor was there, but something unspoken lingered beneath the surface.

"Hey, Alex," I greeted. "How's your week been?"

He shrugged. "Fine, I guess. Classes are busy. Dad called last night. Mom, too. Separate conversations, obviously."

I nodded, waiting for him to continue.

"They keep checking in like they're competing for who gets more updates," he said with a half-laugh, but his eyes betrayed the humor. "It's exhausting."

I waited, holding the space for him.

"I hate my parents."

The words dropped like a stone into a still pond, creating ripples of silence.

Alex began searching my face for judgment. Finding none, he exhaled.

"I really do. I hate them."

"Why?"

His shoulders slumped, and he ran a hand through his hair. "They were so busy proving themselves right—Dad with his 'success isn't everything' speech, Mom clinging to her perfect image of what my future should look like, probably some projected nonsense from her own childhood—that they never thought about what it was doing to me. I spent my whole life trying to **mediate their mess**, and now I feel like I'm still mediating the conflicting voices in my head."

For a moment, the dorm room behind him seemed to fade, leaving only the rawness of his confession.

"Alex," I said, "what's it like carrying all of that anger around?"

He looked down at his hands, clasped tightly in his lap. "It's heavy," he admitted. "But what else am I supposed to do with it? They shaped who I am, for better or worse."

"And yet, you're here," I said. "You're showing up, asking questions, challenging yourself and your own ideas. That tells me you're not just who they made you. You're someone else entirely."

His eyes flicked up to meet mine, uncertain but curious.

"What would life be like for you," I continued, "if you didn't carry that anger anymore?"

Alex stared past the screen, his jaw tightening. "It's not that easy," he said quietly. "I can't just forgive them."

"Forgiveness isn't easy," I agreed. "Carrying that weight might be harder, though."

He didn't respond, but the tension in his posture softened slightly.

"You told me you wanted to get moving, right?" I reminded him. "How can you do that while holding on to this?"

The question hung between us. Finally, Alex spoke, his voice steady but filled with emotion. "I don't know if I can forgive them. Not fully. But I don't want to keep living like this. And you're right—I want to move forward."

I nodded.

Alex nodded back at me slowly, his expression thoughtful. "Maybe . . . maybe it's time to stop holding on."

"Or maybe that pain was never yours to hold," I said, closing our session.

DANNY:

When I arrived at **Danny's garage**, he was waiting at the counter with a small box in hand.

"Hey, Max," he said, sliding it toward me. "Custom air fresheners. Thought you might want one for your car. Fresh leather scent. Premium stuff."

I smirked, picking it up. "Thoughtful. Is this a sales tactic?"

He chuckled, rubbing a grease-streaked hand on his coveralls. "Least I could do the way I spoke to you last time. I know I came off a bit . . . you know."

I smiled. "Direct?"

He smirked. "Yeah, let's call it that. Anyway, I've been thinking about what you said. About trust, leadership, all that. I've made a decision."

We moved to his office, the faint hum of **hydraulic lifts and power tools** filling the air. The rhythm of the shop felt **off—more chaotic than usual, orders being called out with a little more**

edge—but Danny didn't seem to notice. He leaned forward on his desk.

"I want to bring you on to work with the team," he said. "Coach them, train them, whatever you think they need. I'll focus on the bigger picture. We both win."

He paused, locking eyes with me. "This is a big investment, Max. I'm trusting you here, but I need results. And, honestly, I think this is a great opportunity for you too."

I nodded. "Well, thank you for your trust, Danny. But I don't think this will be enough. For lasting change, it has to start with you. **You're the leader. You're the key player of the business.**"

His jaw tightened, and he looked away. **Slowly, he raised his right hand, holding it steady in the air. It was trembling.**

"Do you see this?" he said, his voice low but taut. "This is what it looks like when you're running on fumes. Customers breathing down my neck, parts backordered for months, suppliers screwing me over. I'm trying, Max. I just need some help."

I hesitated, the vulnerability in his voice catching me off guard. "Okay," I said gently. "I'll help you."

He exhaled, his hand dropping back to his lap. "Thanks," he said quietly. Then, almost as if to reassure himself, he muttered, **"It is what it is. We just have to keep pushing."**

As I began working with the team, their frustrations started surfacing.

"He has a great heart," one mechanic said cautiously. "But it's very clear he's got a lot on his shoulders."

Another nodded. "The goalpost keeps moving. We finish

a big repair, and it's, 'Why wasn't it done faster?' 'Why didn't we upsell them?' It's exhausting."

The shop supervisor sighed. "The team's capable, but Danny's stress . . . it spills over. Everything feels like a problem."

Before I could respond, there was a **knock at the office door.**

"Sorry," a junior mechanic said hesitantly. "The diagnostic scanner on Bay Three is **throwing error codes again.**"

I found Danny later, crouched next to the **electrical unit of a lifted SUV**, sleeves rolled up, smudges of grease on his forearm. A ratchet clanged softly as he tightened a bolt.

"Need a hand?" I asked.

He shook his head. "Got it." His voice was clipped, his focus sharp. "Just a patch job. The part's on order."

I watched as he stood, inspecting his work. "You spend a lot of time fixing things yourself?"

"Who else is going to?" He wiped his forehead with the back of his hand. "These cars are everything. If we can't get them back on the road, we're screwed."

He paused, **his gaze drifting across the garage floor**, watching his team move through their tasks. "You know, my dad and my uncles used to **fix everything themselves** back home. Didn't matter if it was a busted truck, a leaking roof, or the boiler in winter. They'd roll up their sleeves and figure it out. That's just what you did."

He leaned down and gave the ratchet one last twist. "That should hold, for now."

His eyes met mine, something raw in his expression. "One thing I haven't really said to you is **thank you.** I know I'm not easy to work with. But I can't let this fail. **I just can't.**"

I extended my hand. He shook it.

Danny's apology, his gratitude, the start of more self-awareness.

We may be getting somewhere.

PRACTICAL EXERCISES

RELEASING THE WEIGHT: FORGIVENESS IN PRACTICE

1. **Identify a Person or Situation**
   - Think of someone you've held resentment towards, or a situation you haven't been able to let go of.
   - It could be a grudge, regret, or unresolved pain—even something minor.
2. **Find a Quiet Space**
   - Go to a space where you can be alone for a while. Bring a notebook or journal.
3. **Write a Letter of Forgiveness**
   - Write a letter to this person (or yourself, if the weight involves guilt or shame). Be radically honest.
     - What did they do?
     - How did it make you feel?
     - How has holding onto this affected your life?
   - Use this closing line:
     "I release this not for them, but for me. I forgive to be free."

4. **Destroy the Letter**
   - Tear it up, burn it (safely), or delete it. The act of letting it go physically symbolizes the emotional release.
5. **Reflect**
   - Write down your immediate thoughts:
     - How did it feel to write the letter?
     - What emotions came up as you destroyed it?
     - Do you feel lighter or more at peace?

FACING THE TRUTH: CONFRONTING MORTALITY

1. **Visit a Cemetery or Quiet, Reflective Spot**
   - Choose a cemetery, a park, or somewhere that reminds you of the passage of time.
   - Sit quietly and observe. Notice the stillness, the names on headstones (if applicable), and the energy of the place.
2. **Write Down These Questions:**
   - If my life ended tomorrow, what would I regret the most?
   - What have I avoided pursuing because of fear or hesitation?
   - What would I do differently if I fully embraced the fact that my time is finite?
3. **Answer with Radical Honesty**
   - In your journal, answer each of the above questions truthfully, without filtering or sugarcoating.
4. **Create a Commitment List**
   - Write down three things you will stop doing today because they don't truly matter.

- Write down three things you will start doing today to honor your finite time.

5. **Take Action**
   - Commit to one small action today to move toward what matters most.
     - Call someone you've been meaning to reconnect with.
     - Begin a project you've been avoiding.
     - Say no to something that doesn't align with your values.

6. **Reflect**
   - After the action, jot down your thoughts:
     - How did it feel?
     - What emotions arose as you confronted mortality head-on?

SO, WHAT'S THE POINT?

Radical honesty puts your feet on firm ground. Forgiveness unties the anchors of the past. Mortality sharpens the priorities of the future.

The runway is clear. Go for it.

THE TOUGH TRUTHS

- You cannot build a meaningful life on top of lies. Embrace radical honesty or stay stuck.
- If you don't clear the baggage, it will keep holding you back.

- Clinging to resentment doesn't hurt them, it only poisons you.
- No one is going to give you permission. You either take action or you don't.
- You will never figure it all out first. Clarity comes from movement, not thought.
- You are running out of time. Plain and simple.
- Act now.

4
WHY DO I EVEN NEED A PURPOSE BEYOND THE SELF?

WAKE-UP CALL

LET'S BEGIN WITH A simple truth: Humans are animals. Like any other creature, we have intrinsic needs that shape how we behave. A dog needs walks, food, play, and affection. Deny these, and the dog suffers. It doesn't matter if it's a Chihuahua or a Great Dane. While every dog is unique, they're still all dogs.

And we are all humans.

Here's the thing: We're not as individual as we'd like to think. While every human being is unique, again, we're all human. So, the question becomes, what does the human animal need?

Connection. Contribution. Community.

For tens of thousands of years, your ancestors lived in tribes. They worked together, shared resources, and protected one another. Alone, they wouldn't have lasted a week. Everything about you—your biology, your brain, your emotions—has been shaped by this reality. Fundamentally, you're wired to find meaning through your role in something larger than yourself.

But here's the problem: We live in environments that don't match what we are intrinsically wired for. We're designed for connection, yet we've built lives of isolation. We're communal by nature, but our culture prizes independence above all else. That's why, when you spend time in nature or with loved ones, you often feel a sense of peace, of oneness with experience. It's not just a coincidence, it's your natural state. And the further we stray from it, the more restless and unfulfilled we become.

Think about it: When you achieve something but have no

one to share it with, how does it feel? Hollow. But when you know in your heart that your actions benefit others, when you share a victory or help someone in need, you feel alive. Have you noticed this? It's not an accident. It's your natural need for connection shining through, if only for a brief moment.

This is why, in practice, a life of "looking after number one" actually doesn't work. The emptiness, the restlessness, the nagging sense of "Is this all there is?"—it's not a flaw in you. It's a sign. A signal that you're going against your own nature.

And this brings us to the great counterintuitive truth about being human: *If you want a better life, stop focusing on you!* The better life you're searching for comes when you align with something beyond you, something that benefits the tribe.

But today, your tribe isn't just your family or neighbors. Your tribe is now the world. The question is no longer, "What will you contribute to your little corner?" It's, "What will you contribute to the world?" We are no longer confined by geography or limited by small communities. In this global age, your actions ripple outward more than ever before, touching lives in ways you will never see.

This is what is meant by a purpose beyond the self. It's not about losing yourself; it's about aligning yourself with the larger story that connects us all. Yes, of course you need your own needs met. But that's the beauty of this path—it's not about sacrifice, but synergy. When you contribute to something greater, you benefit too.

We'll explore those benefits in the next chapter. But for now, understand this: The life you've been searching for, the one that feels truly alive, will never be found through self-obsession.

It's created when you connect outward, when you live for something bigger than yourself.

So, the question becomes:

How do we do this?

DEEPER EXPLORATION

A Purpose Beyond the Self does sound like a bit of an abstract idea, so let's break this down as simply as possible. It's built on three essential components: **Your Gifts, Those You Choose to Serve,** and **A Place to Start.** Together, they form an equation that allows you to live in alignment with your intrinsic nature and find a life of purpose and meaning.

But these components aren't static. They work together dynamically, feeding back into one another, evolving as you do.

Let's take a closer look at each.

Allow this idea to challenge you: **Your Gifts** are not for you. They were never meant to be. You might think of your gifts as personal assets—as skills, talents, or "the stuff that just comes easy to you." But that's a misunderstanding. A gift unshared isn't a gift at all; it's a possession. And possessions, no matter how valuable, grow stagnant when hoarded.

The truth is, your gifts don't exist for your benefit, they exist to serve. Their purpose is realized only when they leave your hands and impact the world. This isn't a suggestion, it's an inherent truth. Think about the word itself: "gift." Its very meaning implies giving. Gifts aren't meant to stay with you;

they're meant to flow through you.

This is the great paradox of the good life: The best way to benefit yourself is to benefit others. And this isn't some abstract new age notion, it's practicality. When your gifts create value for others, that value inevitably flows back to you. The teacher sharpens their understanding through teaching. The entrepreneur thrives by solving a meaningful problem. Contribution serves your own growth because it aligns your actions with your humanity.

The challenge is that your gifts often feel so natural that you might dismiss them. Maybe you have a knack for connecting people, breaking down complex ideas, or spotting beauty in the mundane. Because it comes so effortlessly, you think, *That can't be a big deal.* But that's exactly what makes it your gift—it's meant to flow out of you naturally, to impact others with grace and ease. Your gifts are what you are meant to give away.

The next piece of our equation: **Those You Choose to Serve.** At the risk of repeating myself, let's get something straight: This isn't about saving the world, joining a cause for the sake of appearances, or sacrificing yourself to others. This is about finding where your gifts intersect with the needs of the world in a way that feels meaningful to you.

And the key word here is *feel*.

When you look at the world with radical honesty, pay attention to what grips you. What do you see out there that breaks your heart? These feelings aren't random. They are signals. This is the internal compass of your purpose, pointing you toward the places where your gifts are best served.

Here's the thing: This isn't about logic or strategy, not yet. For now, it's about trust. Trust what moves you. Trust the moments when something grabs you and won't let go. That pull you feel? That's your direction. No one else can feel it for you. No one else can tell you where to go. It has to come from within.

For some of you, this clarity might already be present, a mission that's been quietly waiting for you to notice it. For others, it may take time and self-reflection. Both paths are valid. What matters is this: *This process cannot be outsourced.* No book (including this one), no mentor, no guru can hand you this answer because no one else has access to your experience.

Again, the goal isn't martyrdom; the goal is purpose.

Next, what we need is **A Place to Start**. This is where your gifts and those you choose to serve come to life through action.

Without movement, your purpose remains theoretical.

Drill this into your brain: You don't need a perfect plan. You need a bias toward action. The word "decision" comes from the Latin *decidere*, meaning "to cut off." Every decision you make cuts away other possibilities and forces you to move forward. It's more important to be directionally correct than absolutely correct. Start where you are, with the information you have, and refine as you go. Like a sculptor chiseling away at marble, the shape of your purpose will become clearer with each step you take.

Under no circumstances can you do nothing. Inaction will lead you straight back to the emptiness you've been working to escape, like a rudderless ship getting swept back into shore.

Your gifts, those you choose to serve, and your place to start are not isolated pieces of a puzzle—they are a dynamic, living equation. Your gifts shape who you serve, and as you serve, your understanding of your gifts evolves. As you take action, you'll get feedback, which will clarify direction and reveal opportunities to develop your gifts further and share them more powerfully.

This is how you embody a purpose beyond the self. It's not about perfection or waiting for some magical moment of clarity, it's about the courage to step forward, to begin.

You already know. You've felt it in your gut this entire time.

So the only real question is this: *Are you actually going to do something about it?*

CLIENT STORIES

VANESSA:

Vanessa arrived at our session with her polished exterior intact, but her movements betrayed her unease. She placed her notebook on the table, carefully this time, as though the weight of it mirrored something she wasn't ready to face.

"I almost called it quits," she said abruptly.

"Quits?"

"This," she said, gesturing between us. "The coaching. All of it."

I leaned back slightly, giving her space. "What stopped you?"

Her jaw tightened, and for a moment, she didn't respond. "Anger," she admitted finally. "At you. At myself. At everything."

I stayed silent, waiting.

"After our last session, I couldn't stop thinking about what you said. About my grandmother. About the other grandmothers in those homes who are just . . . **'waiting to die,' as you put it.**"

Her voice was sharper than usual, but beneath it was something more fragile.

"It felt like you were accusing me. Like I was sitting up here in my fancy office, doing nothing, while people like her . . . people like my grandmother, were left to rot."

I remained silent, allowing Vanessa to work through her thoughts.

Her shoulders fell slightly. "I hated it. I hated that you might be right."

She paused, folding her hands tightly on the table. "So I decided the coaching wasn't worth it. That I didn't need someone poking at my life, making me feel worse. I told myself I was too busy anyway, that I had more important things to focus on."

"I see."

She looked down at her hands, fidgeting with a ring on her finger.

"In that case, maybe today can be our last day together," I said, testing her.

The words sat between us, heavy. The sound of the lobby around us disappeared.

"I actually went back to the senior home," she said finally. "I didn't plan to, but I couldn't get it out of my head. I thought maybe I could see it differently, but it was exactly the same. Just as lifeless, just as hollow. And I thought about her, sitting there, **waiting for it all to be over.**"

Her voice broke slightly, but she pressed on. "It's so wrong that people end their lives in places like that." Her gaze lifted to meet mine. "I know there is a way to change that."

I nodded, encouraging her to continue.

"I told myself it's ridiculous. That I don't know anything about running a senior care facility. That I'm too busy, that I don't have the time or the energy. *And the risk, God, the risk.* What if I fail?"

I waited, holding the space for her.

After a moment, she opened her notebook and flipped to a

page covered in neat, precise notes.

"I started writing down ideas," she said, her voice steadier now. "Steps I could take, people I could talk to. **I made a list of questions I need answered.**"

She glanced up at me, a flicker of determination in her eyes.

"And that's enough to start," I said.

Vanessa stood, slipping the notebook into her bag. Her composure had returned, but there was a new edge to it, a quiet resolve.

"This matters," she said, more to herself than to me. She tapped her notebook: *"This actually matters."*

As she walked away, I watched her shoulders straighten with each step. The uncertainty hadn't disappeared, but neither had her determination.

She had made her choice.

The rest would follow.

ALEX:

The screen flickered as Alex welcomed everyone to the Zoom event. I sat quietly among the attendees, my camera off, observing. His energy was unmistakable—a mix of earnestness and nervous anticipation. He had poured everything into this, his first networking session, and it showed in the way he greeted participants and introduced the agenda.

"Thank you all for being here today," he began, his voice steady but tight. "This is a space for meaningful connections, so let's dive in and make it count."

The opening was strong. As the breakout sessions began,

Alex's natural charisma came through. But as the event progressed, the cracks started to show. A tech glitch stranded one group in the main room. Transitions felt rushed. A conversation was cut off mid-sentence when time ran out. None of it was disastrous, but the flow felt uneven.

Still, there were moments. Participants exchanged insights, shared laughs, and found common ground. Alex's effort was evident, and the event wasn't a failure. But as he wrapped up, thanking everyone and asking for feedback, his smile faltered slightly.

After the call, I turned my camera on to debrief. Alex's face appeared, and the buoyant energy from earlier was gone.

"Well," I said, "how are you feeling?"

He exhaled sharply, running a hand through his hair. "Honestly? Like I embarrassed myself."

"What makes you say that?"

He leaned forward, elbows on his knees. "The breakout rooms were a mess. The transitions were awful. I could feel people getting restless." He paused, shaking his head. "This was a mistake."

Before I could respond, his phone buzzed. A chime followed on his computer.

"Feedback's coming in," he said, his voice tense as he opened the responses. His eyes scanned the first submission, and a small smile tugged at his lips. "'Great energy in the group,'" he read. "'Nice way to meet people, thanks Alex.'"

He looked up at me, his confidence lifting slightly. "Not too bad, I guess?"

"Not bad at all," I said.

He kept scrolling. "'Alex's enthusiasm made the session worthwhile.'" His posture straightened. "'Appreciated the breakout rooms for networking.'" The optimism in his voice grew. "Okay, maybe it wasn't all a disaster."

A chime interrupted the moment. Alex opened the latest submission, and his expression hardened. The optimism drained from his face.

"What does it say?" I asked.

"It's from Martin," he said quietly.

Martin. One of his dad's colleagues. A seasoned entrepreneur.

Alex read aloud, "'Alex, I admire your ambition, and it's clear you're passionate about this. But you might want to think about focusing your energy somewhere that plays more to your strengths. Organizing these kinds of events takes a certain finesse, and that's not something everyone has.'"

He set the phone down. "'Not something everyone has...'" he repeated, his voice flat.

"What are you thinking?" I asked.

"He's right," Alex said finally. "Maybe I'm wasting my time."

I waited, watching the weight of the comment settle on him.

"Martin admired your ambition," I said. "He saw your passion. What if this is just the start?"

Alex stared at the screen, silent.

"Alex?"

His eyes met mine, focused.

"I want to try again."

DANNY:

The hum of impact wrenches and air compressors filled the garage as Danny and I sat in his office, the cluttered desk between us a testament to the chaos of the week. Reports, invoices, and half-drunk cups of tea were scattered across the surface, corners curling from hurried handling. Danny leaned back in his chair, arms crossed tightly, his gaze fixed on the performance summary in front of him.

"The numbers are steady," I said, breaking the silence. "The team's doing well."

He shook his head, jaw tightening. "I didn't bring you in for steady, Max. We're not here to be steady. We're here to win."

The edge in his voice wasn't new, but today, it carried something deeper—something unsettled. I let the moment breathe before pressing gently. "You've said that before, Danny. Winning comes up a lot in our conversations—can I ask why winning is so important to you?"

His eyes flicked to me, then dropped to the desk. He was quiet for a moment, the tension in his posture holding like a dam.

"You know where my family's from, right? Proper working-class, Manchester. My dad was a mechanic—his dad was, too. Back home, we didn't have much, just graft and grit." He paused, his hand brushing over a crumpled report on the desk. "When we moved here, we had to prove ourselves. Had to work twice as hard just to be taken seriously."

"And you have," I said softly. "This garage is proof."

He let out a short, bitter laugh. "Is it? Because all I see are the cracks. Margins shrinking. Competition getting tighter.

Customers wanting everything for half the price. And the team . . . not stepping up. I've got a lot riding on this place, Max. I can't let it go under."

The vulnerability in his words was palpable, but before I could respond, he straightened in his chair, pushing the moment away. "Let's just get this meeting over with," he said, his tone hardening. "We've wasted enough time."

The team gathered around the long workbench in the main bay, the air thick with the smell of grease and engine oil. I stood at the front with a notepad, facilitating the workshop Danny had asked me to run. The team engaged cautiously, offering insights and updates, their progress evident but tentative. Danny stood at the edge of the group, arms crossed, his presence heavy. Each comment he made landed like a hammer, tightening the room's energy.

When one of the mechanics mentioned a delay in getting a part installed, Danny interjected sharply. "Why wasn't this sorted sooner?"

The guy hesitated, his voice faltering. "I . . . I thought it was under control."

I stepped in, redirecting the conversation, but the tension lingered. The team pressed on, their contributions hesitant under the weight of Danny's scrutiny.

One of the senior mechanics, his frustration barely contained, muttered under his breath, "Maybe if Danny actually trusted us, we could get on with it."

The room went still. Danny's eyes darkened. His jaw clenched.

For a moment, I thought he might address the comment

directly. Instead, he stepped forward, walking toward the workbench. He paused, his breathing audible, the weight of the room pressing in.

And then it happened.

Danny slammed his fist down onto the metal bench, the impact echoing through the garage like a gunshot. Tools rattled. A few bolts skittered across the floor.

"Enough!" he barked, his voice sharp and unwavering. "If you think you can do it better, go ahead! But don't stand here and tell me I don't trust you when I'm the only one keeping this place running!"

The team froze, their eyes wide with shock. Without another word, Danny turned on his heel and stormed out of the bay, leaving the tension crackling in his wake.

I stood there for a moment, staring at the scattered tools. The silence in the room was deafening, the weight of Danny's outburst settling over everyone.

After the team dispersed, I stayed behind, sitting alone at the workbench. Danny's words echoed in my mind, along with the silence that had followed. The weight of the moment was heavy, but so was the realization it brought.

Danny's drive, his love for the garage, his relentless need to prove himself—it was all undeniable. But so was the toll it was taking. His obsession with control, his inability to let go, was fracturing the very foundation he was trying to build.

The next time I walked into this garage, it wouldn't be to coach Danny.

It would be to end our work together.

PRACTICAL EXERCISES

DISCOVERING YOUR GIFTS—PART 1: HONEST FEEDBACK FROM YOUR TRIBE

Ask the People Who Know You Best

The goal of this exercise is to uncover your natural gifts—the strengths that others see in you, which you might overlook because they come so naturally.

1. **Make a List of 10 People**

   Write down the names of 10 people who know you well. This can include:
   - Family members who've seen you in your most unfiltered moments.
   - Friends who understand your personality and quirks.
   - Colleagues or classmates who've worked closely with you.
   - Mentors, teachers, or supervisors who've observed your growth.
2. **Diversity is key.** Choose people from different parts of your life for a well-rounded perspective.
3. **Ask Them Three Key Questions**

   Reach out to each person. Be clear that you're looking for honest feedback to help you uncover your strengths. Preface with something like:

   "I'm doing an exercise to understand my natural strengths and gifts. I'd really value your input. Please be as honest as possible, I'm

looking for clarity, not compliments."

Then ask:
- *"What do you think I'm naturally good at?"*
- *"When have you seen me at my best?"*
- *"What qualities or strengths do you think set me apart?"*

4. Let them answer freely. If they give a vague response, follow up with curiosity:
   - *"Can you give me an example of when you saw that?"*
   - *"What made that moment stand out to you?"*

5. Listen without Minimizing

   This step is crucial. Resist the urge to downplay their feedback, even if it feels exaggerated or uncomfortable to hear. Pay attention to:
   - The patterns: Which strengths keep coming up?
   - The surprises: Are there gifts they see in you that you don't see in yourself?

6. Be brave enough to accept what they're saying, even if it challenges your self-perception.

7. Write a Summary of Your Gifts

   After gathering the responses, review your notes and identify three to five key gifts. Frame them as clear, actionable statements. For example:
   - *"I create calm in chaos and help others feel grounded."*
   - *"I see connections where others see silos, bringing people and ideas together."*
   - *"I inspire trust and bring out the best in people."*

8. Reflect on Your Summary

   Ask yourself:
   - Do these gifts resonate with me?

- How have I used them in the past?
- What opportunities could I create if I lean into these strengths?

By trusting the insights of those around you, you'll uncover a clearer picture of your gifts. Remember: These are the strengths that come so naturally to you that you may not even recognize them as special. But to others, they are invaluable.

DISCOVERING WHO TO SERVE
Ask Yourself the Big Question
The next step is to connect your gifts to a problem in the world that pulls at you emotionally.

1. Set aside uninterrupted time to journal on the following:
   - *If I could spend my life solving one problem for the world, what would that be?*
   Don't aim for a "perfect" answer—just write whatever comes to mind.
   - *Who are the people most affected by this problem?*
   Picture them. What are their struggles, dreams, and realities?
   - *How could my gifts be of service to them?*
   Look back at your list of gifts. Where do they align with the needs of these people?
2. Choose one small action
   - Don't wait for the "perfect" solution. Choose one small,

specific action to get started. For example:
   i. If your gift is inspiring others, volunteer to lead a group or mentor someone.
   ii. If your gift is problem-solving, offer your skills to a nonprofit or cause you care about.
   iii. If your gift is communication, write or speak about the issue to raise awareness.
3. Commit to acting within the next week. The action doesn't have to be big—it just has to happen.
4. After taking action, journal on the following:
   - How did it feel to connect your gifts to a problem that matters?
   - What did you learn about the people you served? About yourself?
   - What's a next step you can take to build on this momentum?
5. Repeat this process regularly. Each action sharpens your understanding of your purpose.

SO, WHAT'S THE POINT?

You now have a repeatable action plan to hone in on your purpose. By making the commitment to re-engaging in Chapters Three and Four, you'll find it—it's just a matter of how long it will take. But you'll be surprised how often your purpose is hiding in plain sight.

THE TOUGH TRUTHS

- You are not as independent as you think. Your shared humanity connects you to those around you.
- A life built solely around yourself will never be enough, no matter how much you achieve.
- The emptiness you feel is not a mystery, it's a signal that you are living out of alignment with your biological nature.
- Your talents and gifts were never meant to be hoarded—they only have value when offered to someone else.
- The world does not owe you purpose—you must step forward and claim it.
- You are not lost. You are disconnected.

5
WHAT'S IN IT FOR ME?

WAKE-UP CALL

LET'S CLEAR SOMETHING UP right now: *This isn't a book about changing careers.*

If you're still thinking, "Oh, cool, this is a guide to finding a more fulfilling job," you've missed the point entirely. This is about something much bigger. Something far more powerful.

Until now, we've explored the deeper currents that shape your life—culture, history, human nature. And while all of it is true, it may have felt distant, abstract, even grandiose. But now, we're bringing it back full circle.

It's time to ask the question that's been quietly sitting in the background all along:

What's in it for you?

Not for the world. Not for humanity at large. But for **You**. For your individual life.

Here's the thing you need to grasp before we go any further:

No part of your life exists in isolation.

Your career impacts your relationships. Your mental health impacts your physical health. The fulfillment from your friendships impacts your work. Every part of your life is interconnected, whether you see it or not.

Think about it: When one piece of your life is out of alignment, doesn't it spill into everything else?

Stress from work shows up in your marriage. Exhaustion makes you short-tempered with your friends and colleagues. That nagging sense of emptiness might even have you reaching for a drink after work, just to take the edge off. It's all connected.

And when you bring yourself into alignment with your true

nature, you will finally find the good life. Without a doubt.

But before we explore that, let's pause for a moment and confront a deeper question:

What is "the good life," anyway?

For decades, you've been sold an image: The good life is sipping margaritas on a beach under the Jamaican sun, without a care in the world. Sounds nice, right?

As nice as it sounds, that image is dangerous. In fact, it's a trap. It's the dangling carrot that keeps you running on the infamous treadmill we've talked about, believing that if you just work hard enough, save enough, climb high enough, you'll finally be able to kick back and relax.

Besides, here's the reality of that idyllic vacation vision: The first three days? Sure, it'd be nice. Two weeks in, you'd be restless. Three weeks in, bored out of your mind. Three months later, you'd be miserable . . . and probably an alcoholic.

The truth is, **you're not built for comfort.**

You're built for **adventure.** For **challenge.** For **depth.**

You thrive when you're engaged. When your actions matter. When you're connected to something that pulls you forward, when you're living on the edge of something bigger, something greater. The good life isn't found in comfort, it's found in purpose.

And here's the deep irony:

With a life of purpose, you'll be more successful than ever before—not to mention more fulfilled than ever, too.

We'll dive deeper into this shortly, but suffice it to say, the benefits of embracing your purpose are not just universal—they're personal. They're immediate. And they're profound.

So, what's in it for you?

Let's find out.

DEEPER EXPLORATION

This book has done everything possible to avoid exaggeration, and nowhere is that more important than here. It would be easy to overstate the ideas in this chapter, but that would be doing you a disservice. So, please understand that the benefits of embracing a purpose beyond the self have been laid out to you with very careful consideration.

This chapter is about you. Please take this seriously.

Let's start with your health. Have you ever wondered why it feels so hard to stick to healthy habits? Why does the pull toward junk food, social media, or other distractions feel so strong? It's not a lack of discipline. It is often said that addictions, no matter how hard or soft they are, are not the problem, they are the solution. So, what are they the solution for? Most fundamentally, they provide temporary solace from the discomfort of a life that feels misaligned. When you're stuck in a cycle of chronic dissatisfaction, unhealthy habits become the easiest way to cope.

When your life aligns with your intrinsic nature, that need to escape starts to fade. It's not that you become a health guru, it's that those indulgences just feel different. They're no longer a crutch, but a choice. You might still enjoy some junk food, unwind with a good Netflix series, have a social drink on the odd occasion, but it's something you do because you want to, not because you're numbing yourself. Things don't become effortless per se, but they become natural. The constant tension of fighting with yourself fades, replaced by a sense of ease.

Speaking of relief, one of the most subtle but profound benefits is freedom from self-obsession. Most of us spend an embarrassing amount of time in our own heads. Think about how much mental energy you waste replaying conversations, worrying if you came across as smart or funny enough, or crafting the perfect response to an argument that happened two weeks ago. It's a bit petty, isn't it? (Not to mention, exhausting.)

When you're focused on something bigger than yourself, all that noise fades. You stop being the star of your own soap opera. You step out of the cramped theater of your mind and into the open air. There's space now, and you can really breathe.

Confidence is another piece of the puzzle. When you inhabit a purpose beyond yourself, confidence stops being something you fake. You don't need to Google "self-esteem hacks" like "smile at yourself for three minutes in the mirror." The evidence of your own life will tell you that you're someone worth respecting. Seeing the meaningful impact you make and knowing your actions matter creates real confidence. It's not something you have to convince yourself of; it's someone that you are.

Even suffering takes on new meaning. Let's be honest here: Life is hard no matter what path you choose. The question becomes, what is your suffering in service of? There's an enormous difference between suffering under the weight of petty concerns and carrying a burden that's worth it. When your struggles are tied to something bigger than yourself, they don't feel pointless. They feel meaningful. They shape you, strengthen you, and make you better. Then, whatever burden you're carrying becomes a privilege.

For those of you with kids, here's something to consider: This shift will make you a better parent, too. When you live a life of alignment, your children see that. They see a parent who is energized, present, and fulfilled. They see what it looks like to live a life of purpose in their own home, which is one of the most powerful lessons you could ever teach them.

Now onto a huge elephant in the room: Money. When you create real value in the world, you deserve to get paid.

You might think choosing a purpose that means something to you is a path to the poorhouse, but the truth is that aligning your gifts with solving meaningful problems isn't just fulfilling; it's incredibly valuable. The marketplace rewards those who bring value, plain and simple. When you've found and are aligned with your purpose, your output skyrockets. Your ideas resonate, your energy is contagious, and people want to work with you. That's the kind of value that commands attention—and yes, compensation.

Here's the paradox: You'll likely earn more than ever before, yet it won't matter to you in the same way. Money becomes a byproduct, not the purpose. Your whole relationship with money changes. It no longer represents a ticket to escape your pain; instead, it becomes a tool to serve your mission. And yes, you can indulge now and again with a nice trip to Jamaica—but the truth is, even that desire may fade.

Now to our most profound point: **The most important benefit is who you become.** When you align with a purpose beyond the self, you are quite literally becoming the person you're meant to be. You know all those empty personal development platitudes about becoming your authentic self and realizing your potential? Well, this is what that actually looks like—not as a marketing gimmick, but as a lived reality. You won't need to convince yourself you're fulfilled. You'll know.

Sure, this path is about making the world better. But equally as importantly, it's about making your life better. Tangibly. Meaningfully. Profoundly.

Align yourself with something real, and everything changes.

CLIENT STORIES

VANESSA:

The view from Vanessa's home office was striking, a sweeping panorama of the city skyline bathed in the golden hues of late afternoon light. It was a space that spoke volumes about her—polished yet thoughtful, understated yet undeniably successful. As she welcomed me in, there was a new energy about her, a balance between quiet focus and intense determination.

"Thanks for coming, Max," she said, leading me through to her office. "I needed a break from the noise."

I followed her into a space that mirrored her personality: Precise, intentional, and meticulously organized. Papers were stacked neatly, a leather-bound notebook lay open on the desk, and her laptop hummed softly in the background. She gestured toward the chair across from her, settling into her own seat with a sigh.

"The office can be . . . suffocating," she admitted. "Here, I can actually breathe and focus. Between the consultancy, the senior home project, and my time with the family, I feel like I'm juggling three lives."

The senior home. It was no longer just an idea—it had become real. She opened her laptop and pulled up the proposal, her expression softening as she glanced at the screen. "I wanted to run these numbers by you. There's a lot riding on this, and I need to get it right."

As she walked me through her plan, her precision and

intellect were undeniable. Every detail of the budget had been scrutinized, every assumption backed with data. The same sharp analytical mind that had made her a force in the corporate world was now being leveraged for something far more personal and meaningful.

"What do you think your grandmother would say?" I asked as she finished.

She paused, her gaze lingering on the screen. "I hope she'd be proud," she said softly. "This feels . . . different. My consulting work is fine, but this feels real."

There was a vulnerability in her words that hadn't been there in our earlier sessions.

"And how's the balance?" I asked.

She leaned back, her eyes drifting to the skyline. "It's hard. The late nights, the early mornings . . . the kids have noticed. My husband's been supportive, but I can tell he's worried. He thinks I'm pushing too hard."

"Do you think he's right?"

She hesitated, then nodded slightly. "Probably. But then I think about what I'm teaching my kids, the example I'm setting. Some things are worth the effort."

"You're setting an incredible example," I said.

Her lips curved into a small, wry smile. "That's the hope. I just need to make this proposal land. If I can secure the funding, it's game over. I can work out the rest."

For the next hour, we refined the proposal. She tightened the language, clarified the numbers, and adjusted her pitch. As I watched her work, it struck me how far she'd come. This wasn't just about honoring her grandmother or creating something for the community. It was about Vanessa becoming a woman unafraid of her own greatness.

As I stood to leave, she walked me to the door.

"Thanks for coming, Max," she said.

"You're welcome," I replied.

She nodded, her eyes resolute. "Friday's the deadline."

I held her gaze for a moment, sensing her quiet determination.

"I'm ready," she said.

ALEX:

Alex's face appeared on the screen, framed by a backdrop of trees and open sky. He was sitting on a park bench, the sunlight filtering through the branches above. A small fountain glimmered in the distance, just visible over his shoulder. The scene was a stark contrast to his usual dorm room.

"Nice view today," I noted.

Alex glanced over his shoulder and gave a faint smile. "Yeah. Figured a change of scenery couldn't hurt. Needed some space to think."

There was something different about him.

He leaned forward, his hands clasped in front of him. "I've been thinking a lot since the last event. About the feedback, about Martin's comment . . ." He hesitated, glancing down before meeting my gaze. "I think I've been trying to force myself into a mold that doesn't fit me."

I nodded, waiting for him to continue.

"It's like this: My dad's always encouraged me to go big, like he did. And my mom's always encouraged me to make money, because that's the life she's always wanted for herself. But the truth is, that's actually not who I am." He straightened in his chair, his voice steady. "What stuck with me after the event wasn't Martin's comment. It was the positive feedback. People said I made them feel heard. That I brought them together. And you know what, Max? That's it. That's where I shine."

I smiled. "So what's next?"

Alex's face lit up with a flicker of excitement. "No overcomplicated agendas, no big expectations. Just a handful of people, connecting on a real level."

Two weeks later, Alex hosted his second networking session, a small, informal meetup with five attendees. This time, the approach was intentional. He invited participants with overlapping interests, people who wouldn't normally cross paths but had something meaningful to share with one another.

The session began with a simple icebreaker: "What's a challenge in your industry that keeps you up at night?" Alex listened attentively, his eyes lighting up as the conversation flowed. When someone hesitated, he offered a gentle nudge. When two attendees found a shared challenge, Alex stepped back, letting their dialogue unfold naturally.

It wasn't perfect. But it was leaps and bounds stronger than his first attempt. By the end, it was clear the session had left an impact. Attendees lingered long after it officially ended, exchanging contact details and making plans to collaborate.

As the Zoom room finally emptied, Alex leaned back in his chair, a quiet smile on his face. This wasn't just an event. It was a step toward something meaningful.

A few days later, Alex called me.

"So, I told my mom about it," he said.

I waited.

"She doesn't get it," he continued, his voice flat. "She kept asking how I'm going to make it work. How I'm going to make money."

"And what did you say?" I asked.

"I told her I don't know yet." He paused, his gaze drifting somewhere off-screen. "She said she's worried. That she just wants me to be okay."

The silence hung between us.

"And how do you feel about that?" I asked.

There was a shift in his voice now. Steady. Certain.

"It'll be fine," he said.

DANNY:

I sat in Danny's office, the weight of my mistake settling in. Agreeing to work with his team had been the wrong call. His drive and control weren't just holding them back. They were breaking them.

This was going to be a hard conversation.

Danny paced, his footsteps heavy against the concrete floor. His desk was buried under invoices, supply orders, and notes scrawled in frustration.

"Max," he said abruptly. "I can't just stop pushing. Not now. Not when we're this close to turning things around."

"Danny," I said, "you're driving yourself into the ground. And the team . . . they're at their breaking point too."

He stopped pacing, turning to face me. His eyes burned with frustration. "They don't get it. None of them do. This isn't just a garage. This is everything my dad worked for. Everything I've worked for. You think I can just sit back and let it fall apart?"

"You're not sitting back," I said gently. "But you are pushing so hard that—"

The sharp smell of smoke hit my nose. Danny noticed it too. His head snapped toward the shop floor.

"Do you smell that?" I asked.

He nodded, already moving. When he threw open the office door, smoke poured in, thick and black.

"Fire!" someone shouted from the main floor.

Danny bolted. I followed. Flames were licking up the side of a hydraulic lift, fueled by spilled oil and rags. The smoke was suffocating, the heat unbearable.

"Everyone out!" I yelled. The team hesitated, their eyes darting to Danny.

"Go!" he barked. "Get outside now!"

The team scrambled for the exit. I grabbed Danny's arm, but he yanked free.

"I'm not leaving!" he shouted. "This is my place!"

"Danny, you can't."

He didn't listen. He grabbed an extinguisher and aimed it at the flames. The spray barely made a dent. The fire spread faster, climbing the walls and swallowing the machinery.

I ran outside to check on the team. They were coughing, pale-faced, huddled in the parking lot.

"Stay here," I said, before rushing back inside.

The heat hit me like a wall. Danny was still there, coughing, struggling to fight the flames.

"Danny!" I shouted. He didn't turn.

"Go, Max!" he yelled. "I've got this!"

He didn't. The fire was everywhere now. Smoke filled the shop, thick and blinding.

Sirens wailed. The fire brigade arrived, their lights flashing red and blue. I pointed frantically. "He's still in there!"

They moved fast, disappearing into the smoke. Minutes dragged like hours. Finally, two firefighters emerged, dragging Danny between them.

His face was blackened with soot, his coveralls singed, his body limp.

They carried him to the parking lot. I stepped forward, catching him as he collapsed into my arms.

"It's gone," he rasped. "Everything . . . gone."

His eyes were hollow and bloodshot, his body sagging against me. But he was still breathing.

As the firefighters worked and the team stood in shock, I stayed with Danny, his weight heavy in my arms, his breaths shallow.

The fire wasn't just consuming the building. It was consuming him. And I could feel his devastation in every broken breath.

The flames raged on, devouring everything in their path.

Danny's eyes met mine.

"I'm sorry, Max."

"I'm sorry too, Danny…"

PRACTICAL EXERCISES

PART 1: DEFINING A GOOD LIFE FOR YOU

Create Your "Good Life" Categories
List five areas of your life where you want to experience alignment and growth. Examples:
- Career
- Relationships
- Health
- Personal Growth
- Finances

Envision Alignment in Each Area
For each category, ask yourself:
- What does alignment look like for me here?
- How would finding a purpose beyond myself improve this part of my life?

Write a short goal for each category.

Examples:
- Career: "Using my strengths to solve problems I care about, where I feel energized and valued."
- Relationships: "Being more present and connected because I'm no longer consumed by stress or self-doubt."

Write Your "Good Life" Statement

Combine your reflections into a single sentence summarizing your good life.

Example:
- "The good life for me means using my gifts to contribute meaningfully to the world, while living in alignment with my values and being present for the people I love."

PART 2: BRINGING IT BACK TO YOU

Identify One Key Gift That Feels Rewarding to Use

Look back at your gifts from earlier chapters. Pick one that:

- Feels most enjoyable or natural to use.
- Gives you a sense of pride, joy, or accomplishment when you apply it.

Write it down.

Example:
- "I'm great at simplifying complex ideas, and it feels rewarding when people tell me I made something easier for them to understand."

Choose One Context That Benefits You

Ask: Where can I use this gift in a way that creates value for others while giving me something in return?

Options:

1. **Your Career:**
   - Could you use this gift to improve your performance, reputation, or position?
   - Example: "Simplifying complex ideas could help me present solutions more clearly in meetings, making me stand out as a leader."
2. **Your Personal Life:**
   - How could this gift improve your relationships or emotional well-being?
   - Example: "If I explain things better at home, I could reduce tension and improve communication with my family."
3. **Your Growth or Exploration:**
   - How could this gift help you learn, grow, or open new doors?
   - Example: "Using this skill to write an article or share ideas online could build confidence or create opportunities."

Create a Contribution Experiment

Design a small action that directly benefits you.

Ask yourself:
- What do I want to get out of this action? (Recognition, clarity, growth, emotional relief.)
- How can I use my gift to create something that feels immediately rewarding?

Examples:
- **Recognition:** Offer to take on a task at work that highlights your gift, like creating a presentation or solving a problem.
- **Emotional Relief:** Use your gift to resolve a personal issue, like organizing a chaotic space or addressing a conflict.
- **Opportunities:** Share your gift with a wider audience—write, teach, or collaborate on something that puts you in the spotlight.

Reflect on the Outcome

After completing the action, journal on these questions:

1. What did I gain? (Be specific: Did you feel more confident, energized, or respected?)
2. What tangible results came from this action? (Recognition, feedback, or a new opportunity?)
3. How did this action connect to my deeper sense of purpose?
4. How can I refine and repeat this process to create more rewards for myself?

SO, WHAT'S THE POINT?

Each time you go through these exercises, it'll bring you closer to the good life, where your strengths create rewards, both tangible and emotional, that flow naturally back to you. It's a cycle worth repeating.

THE TOUGH TRUTHS

- You don't need a bigger pay check or a better title, you need a powerful reason to get out of bed in the morning.
- No amount of money will make up for a life that feels empty, ever.
- The pursuit of comfort is the fastest route to misery.
- The greatest confidence boost doesn't come from self-affirmation, it comes from undeniable results in the real world.
- You will suffer no matter what. The only choice is whether your suffering is in the service of something meaningful.
- Your purpose isn't a "nice thing to have"—it's the foundation everything else rests on.

What the F*ck Do You Actually Want?

6
CALLING ME A HERO IS A BIT MUCH, ISN'T IT?

WAKE-UP CALL

LET ME SAY IT plainly: You are a hero in the making.

Maybe this feels like an overreach. Heroes, you may tell yourself, are the ones who do extraordinary things. They sacrifice everything. They fight battles on grand stages. Their names end up in history books.

But heroes aren't born into greatness. They don't come with special gifts or perfect timing. What separates heroes from everyone else is this: Even when it's hard, even when they don't have all the answers, they choose to strive for what's right. They show up big when it would be easier to stay small.

Striving for good comes down to a decision, in the face of everything broken, that you're still going to make things better where you can.

And whether you've realized it yet or not, you've already heard the call.

You know the feeling: That pull. That quiet voice that whispers, *"There's more in you here."* That moment when you see something that needs fixing and feel the urge to step in, even if you don't know how. That's the call to strive for good, and it's one that most people ignore.

Why? Most simply, because it's easier not to.

It's easier to focus on yourself, to numb out, to stay small and comfortable. The world often rewards us for doing exactly that, for playing the game and keeping our heads down. But here's the thing: **The world doesn't move forward on its own.** It moves forward because of those who carry it forward, refusing to let it stall.

Not perfect people. Not powerful people. But people who

choose to try anyway. These are the heroes.

And this is you.

Think about it: You're still here. Still reading. Still searching. That alone says something about who you are. Somewhere deep down, you know you're capable of more. You know you can be part of something bigger, something better. Even if you don't have the whole map yet, you're willing to take the first step.

That's what makes a hero.

Because striving for good, no matter how small it starts, matters. A kind word, a generous act, a problem solved, a gift shared. It all matters more than you might ever realize. Goodness spreads. It creates ripples that become waves. And all waves, no matter how big or small, reshape the shore. You may not see the full impact of what you do, but I promise you this: When you choose to show up, the world is changed.

All you need is a willingness to say, *"I'll do what I can, with what I have, right now."*

That's it. That's the difference.

And here's the beauty of striving for good: It doesn't just impact the world. It brings forward the best in you. It makes you stronger, braver, and more alive. It brings depth and meaning to your life in ways that chasing survival can't.

So yes, calling you a hero might feel like too much. But it's not.

A hero is simply someone who strives for good, even when the outcome is uncertain. Someone like you.

The call has come. It's here, right now, in front of you. Take it.

DEEPER EXPLORATION

The world is incredibly complex, and yet most people agree on one thing: They see themselves as fundamentally good. Yes, we all have complicated relationships with ourselves, but when pressed, most people would argue that beneath our doubts, fears, and flaws, we are fundamentally decent. Few wake up in the morning with the intent to harm others or contribute to the world's problems. And yet, the state of the world speaks for itself. It's a crucial question for us to answer here: If everyone fundamentally sees themselves as good, how is it possible that so much suffering, division, inequality, and pain persist?

The answer lies in our quiet detachment. Most people recognize that the world could do with a dose of improving, but the sheer size and complexity of the world's problems feel overwhelming. What could I possibly do? Faced with this enormity, it is easier to retreat to what feels manageable: Your career, your family, and your personal goals. This isn't evil; it's human. But it creates a paradox. When billions of people believe they are not part of the problem, no one steps up to be part of the solution. The result? The world continues on, its problems intact.

And yet, the world doesn't improve on its own. Change doesn't come from the masses. It comes from the few who have the courage to care—and, more importantly, the courage to act. These aren't perfect people, nor are they extraordinary. The difference is actually very simple. They are simply willing to try. That is what separates heroes from everyone else. Not some grand birthright or supernatural gift, but the decision to show up and strive for good, even in the face of uncertainty.

This is why you are a potential hero. But let's take a moment to clarify what that means. A hero isn't someone with a cape or laser-beam eyes. A hero is simply someone who chooses to expand their love and vision beyond themselves. The difference between a hero and a villain is not in their origin story. It's who they choose to be *now*. It is in the scope of their vision. Both heroes and villains often emerge from uncannily similar beginnings: Pain, rejection, and a desire to change their circumstances. But while a hero's vision includes others, a villain's vision begins and ends with their own needs. And when you think about it, how many people today live with aspirations that serve only their small circle? Villainy, in this context, isn't about evil. It is simply a love that is limited to a small circle.

Heroes, by contrast, touch us emotionally. They remind us of what we could be. When we watch Frodo, Neo, or Harry Potter rise to their challenges, we aren't just entertained. We're moved. Because in their journeys, we see a reflection of our own potential to stand for something greater. Heroes inspire us because they remind us that a life spent striving for good is not only meaningful but deeply possible.

And striving for good creates ripples. Let's pause here to define what ripples are, as this is a crucial concept. Every choice you make, no matter how small, sends ripples outward. A moment of kindness, an encouraging word, or a simple act of patience doesn't just stop with the person in front of you, it carries forward. The impact spreads, often in ways you'll never see, influencing the world beyond your reach.

Think about it: You offer a moment of genuine kindness to someone—a friend, a colleague, or even a stranger. You lift their spirits with a word of encouragement, giving them the energy to approach their day differently. They, in turn, show unexpected patience to someone else who is struggling, who then carries that moment forward into their own life. And just like that, the ripple grows, often unseen, but undeniably real.

Rosa Parks didn't set out to change the world. She simply stayed in her seat because her conscience told her it was the right thing to do. Yet that one small decision rippled outward, becoming a catalyst for seismic change. The truth is, you have no idea what your ripples are capable of. Your job isn't to save the world. It is to take deep responsibility for the ripples that you create, and then to create them as powerfully as you can.

But the question remains: Why don't more people choose this path? The answer is simple. Fear. Fear of failure, of judgment, of insignificance. Fear of what your family will think. Fear of stepping into the unknown. It is easier to play it safe, to stay in your comfort zone, and to believe that one person can't possibly make a difference. But here's the deep irony. The world changes precisely because ordinary people decide to try. Heroes don't start as heroes. Frodo was a simple hobbit. Neo was asleep in the Matrix. Harry Potter lived in a cupboard under the stairs. Peter Parker was a geeky teenager ignored by the world. And here's a key truth to remember: None of them knew how their journeys would end. They didn't feel ready, and neither do you. But they accepted the call anyway.

And this is where we come to the beginning of your journey. You don't need to have all the answers. You don't need to feel certain. You simply need to make a decision to start. The question isn't whether you can make a difference. The question is whether you'll choose to try.

At the end of your life, when you look back, you won't measure your success by the number of things you owned or the accolades you collected. You'll measure it by the lives you touched. You'll ask yourself one simple question: Was the world better because I was in it? And the answer will depend on the kind of ripples you chose to create.

Your life matters. Your actions matter. Yes, the world is complicated, and the problems we face are immense, as they always have been. But the solution doesn't lie in waiting for someone else to fix them. It lies in people like you taking ownership of the good you can create with the gifts you've been given—and trusting that this good will spread.

You are a hero in the making. Not because you're destined or special. But because every act of goodness counts.

Nobody's handing you a cape.

You don't need one.

Just step the fuck up.

CLIENT STORIES

VANESSA:

The conference room was harshly lit, the kind of lighting that sharpened every detail, leaving no space to hide. Vanessa sat at the far end of the long, imposing table, the only woman in a sea of dark suits and carefully measured expressions. The funding board members sat stiffly, their untouched copies of her proposal laid neatly in front of them, each member radiating quiet authority.

The air hummed with tension, a silent reminder that this room held the power to make or break her vision.

She had spent years preparing for high-stakes meetings like this, but this time was different. This wasn't about maximizing profits or delivering for the firm. This was about something real. Something that mattered.

A home where people like her grandmother—people who had given their whole lives to their families and communities—could live their final years with dignity, joy, and purpose.

The questions came hard and fast.

"What's your experience in this sector?"

"What's the long-term sustainability model?"

"Isn't this a high-risk venture given your lack of direct expertise?"

That last one came from a man near the end of the table, his tone sharp, dismissive. The kind of question designed to make her falter.

Vanessa met his gaze without hesitation. "I've spent my entire career managing high-risk ventures. I know what it takes to build something that lasts. And I know that the greatest risk is doing nothing—letting people like my grandmother waste away in places that strip them of their humanity."

Silence stretched through the room.

The board members exchanged glances, their expressions unreadable. She had seen this before, in negotiations where millions of dollars hung in the balance. But this time, she wasn't just fighting for numbers on a balance sheet.

She was fighting for something bigger than herself.

Minutes dragged by. Then finally, one of the senior members cleared his throat. "We'll be in touch with final details, but . . . welcome aboard."

Approval.

For a moment, she just sat there, the weight of it settling in.

Then, slowly, she nodded, standing with quiet certainty.

By the time she stepped out into the hallway, her hands were steady, but her breath felt different—lighter. I was waiting outside, leaning casually against the wall.

When her eyes met mine, the polished exterior cracked just slightly, enough to reveal the quiet elation of someone who had just stepped across a threshold.

"They said yes," she whispered, her voice barely audible but brimming with restrained emotion.

The world outside the conference room hadn't changed. The hum of distant office chatter continued. But as Vanessa walked past me, her head was held high and her shoulders were straighter than I'd ever seen.

It was clear. *Everything* **had changed.**

ALEX:

I met Alex in a café near his campus, the late afternoon sunlight streaming through the tall windows, casting golden hues across the room. He was already at a corner table, a notebook open in front of him, its edges filled with scribbled notes and bold ideas.

When he looked up and saw me, he grinned—a calm, confident smile that carried none of the restless energy I had once associated with him. I was in town for a session with his dad, and this was the first time Alex and I had met face to face.

"Max," he said warmly, standing to greet me. His handshake was firm yet easy, his movements relaxed. There was something different about him now, a quiet self-assurance that spoke of lessons learned and growth hard-earned.

We ordered coffee and sat down. As we caught up, Alex reflected on how much had shifted over the past months. His networking events had evolved—not just in size, but in depth. Instead of fixating on numbers or scale, he had refined his approach, prioritizing meaningful conversations over impressive spectacles. Word had spread, and professionals far beyond his original circle were now reaching out, eager to be part of what he had built.

"What's changed the most," he said, pausing to choose his words, "is that I've stopped trying to prove something. I realized it's not about being perfect or impressive. All I had to do was create spaces where people feel seen, valued, and connected. And I've finally embraced that I'm good at that."

He leaned back in his chair, his expression thoughtful. "I guess I stopped fighting who I am. And once I did, everything just started working."

It wasn't just the words—it was how he said them. There was no hesitation, no self-doubt, no need for validation. Alex wasn't the same person I had met months ago.

Then, in the middle of our conversation, his phone buzzed on the table. He glanced at the screen, his eyebrows raising slightly. Without a word, he slid the phone toward me.

The sender was Martin. The same Martin who, months earlier, had dismissed Alex with cutting feedback. The message read:

Alex, I wanted to apologize for my earlier comments. I underestimated you, and I was wrong. What you're building is something special, and I'd love the chance to be part of it. If there's space, I'd like to attend your next event.

I looked up at Alex. He met my gaze, calm and steady. There was no flicker of the old restlessness, no trace of the need for vindication that had once fueled him.

"What will you say?" I asked.

Alex smiled—the kind of smile that comes from someone completely at home in themselves.

"I'll tell him he's very welcome."

And with that, his notebook still open beside him, Alex leaned back in his chair, emanating the quiet confidence of someone who had stepped fully into his strengths—and into the world.

DANNY:

The café was bustling with the morning rush, the hum of conversation mingling with the hiss of steaming milk and the clatter of cups. I spotted Danny immediately, tucked into a corner table, staring down at a black coffee.

I walked over, and Danny looked up, offering a faint smile. "Max," he said, gesturing to the chair across from him. "Thanks for coming."

I sat down, the weight of the envelope in my pocket a constant reminder of why I was here. Danny looked different. The once unshakable intensity in his eyes had softened, replaced by something quieter, more subdued.

"How are you holding up?" I asked.

He shrugged, his expression inscrutable. "I've had better months."

A waiter approached, notebook in hand. Before I could say anything, Danny glanced up and said, "Put his order on me. Least I can do—I know I've put you through a lot too."

It was a simple gesture, but it carried a weight that words couldn't. Even in the wreckage of everything he'd lost, Danny's heart was still intact.

After we ordered, I leaned forward slightly. "You've been through hell, Danny. That's not easy for anyone. Have you thought about what comes next?"

He sighed, running a hand over his face. "Not much choice, is there? Gotta rebuild."

I reached into my pocket and pulled out the envelope, placing it on the table between us. Danny frowned, his eyes flicking from the envelope to me.

"What's this?" he asked.

"It's a refund," I said simply. "For the work we did together. The outcomes didn't come to fruition. And I can't, in good conscience, hold onto it."

Danny stared at the envelope for a moment, then back at me. "Max, you don't have to do this. None of this was your fault."

"I know," I said. "But the truth is, I missed something too. I thought we could turn it around. I believed in the work we were doing, and I still do. But I also see now that maybe . . . maybe it wasn't time yet. And that's on me."

For a moment, Danny didn't say anything. Then he reached out and slid the envelope back across the table toward me.

"Keep it," he said firmly. "You earned it. You tried to help me, Max. You gave me every opportunity to turn this around. I just . . . I wasn't there yet."

I hesitated, then pushed the envelope back toward him. "It's yours, Danny. Use it for whatever comes next. Build something new."

He looked at me for a long moment, his jaw tightening. "I'll think about it," he said, his voice low. "But honestly, Max, I don't even know where to start."

"That's okay," I said gently. "The fire wasn't the end, Danny. It was a beginning. You just have to decide what you want to build next."

I saw something flicker in his eyes, something fragile and fleeting, like a shadow of hope. But then it was gone, replaced by the familiar armor I'd seen him wear so many times before.

"What would you do differently?" I asked softly, leaning forward. "If you could start fresh?"

He looked down at his coffee, stirring it absently. For a moment, I thought he might finally let the armor crack.

But instead, he shrugged, his voice steady but distant. "It is what it is, Maxie. I've just gotta keep pushing."

The words landed heavily between us. He said them with a half-smile, as if trying to convince himself they were enough. I forced a small smile in return, but inside, I felt the ache of it.

Because Danny was a good man. A deeply good man. And yet, even now, even with everything laid bare, he couldn't let go of the very mindset that had brought him here.

As I stood to leave, Danny reached out and shook my hand firmly. "Thanks, Max," he said quietly. "For everything."

I nodded, meeting his gaze. "Take care of yourself, Danny."

He gave me a faint smile, but his eyes drifted back to the coffee in front of him.

As I walked away, something in me sank. This was the worst outcome in my career by a long way.

I wanted to tell him he didn't have to keep pushing. That there was another way. That he could rebuild not just his garage but his approach, his purpose, his life. But I knew Danny wasn't ready to hear it. Not yet.

As I walked out of the café, I couldn't help but think about how much potential Danny had. His grit, his loyalty to his family's legacy, his drive—they were all pieces of something bigger, waiting to come together. But the same qualities that made Danny who he was also kept him stuck.

For now, though, his story ends here—a reminder that even the best of us can stay trapped when we don't heed the call to change.

PRACTICAL EXERCISES

PART 1: A HERO'S COMMITMENT TO DISCOVERY AND CONTRIBUTION

This journey is not about a quick fix or a small, isolated act. It's about committing to uncovering, aligning with, and embodying your Purpose Beyond the Self—a purpose that evolves with you as you take action and grow.

Step 1: Write Your Commitment

Take time to craft a statement that represents your vow aligning your life and your purpose. Use these prompts to guide you:

- What am I committing to discovering?
- What kind of impact do I want to create, even if I don't have all the answers yet?
- What am I willing to give of myself in service of something greater?

Examples:

- "I commit to a lifelong journey of discovering and embodying my Purpose Beyond the Self—even if it takes time, and even if it's uncomfortable."
- "I vow to create a meaningful legacy by contributing my gifts to the world and living in alignment with my values."
- "I dedicate myself to continuously refining my purpose

and expanding the impact of my life, however far that may take me."

Step 2: Envision Your Legacy

Imagine yourself ten years into the future. You've been living a life of purpose, with all the inherent benefits of such an existence coming back to you and more. Ask yourself:

- What did I need to realize about myself that sparked the turning point in my life?
- What was the greatest fear that I overcame about myself?
- What have I created, and who has benefited because I chose this path?

Write down your answers. Let your imagination run free. Focus not on the specifics of what you've done, but on the impact and alignment you've achieved.

PART 2: THE PRACTICE OF REFINING AND LIVING YOUR PURPOSE

Your Purpose Beyond the Self isn't static. It will shift as you grow, as the world changes, and as your understanding deepens. The following practice is designed to help you stay aligned, sharpen your clarity, and live your purpose fully.

Step 1: Set a Regular Reflection Practice

Once a month (or at an interval that feels right to you), reflect on these questions:

- How have I moved into my Purpose Beyond the Self this month?
- Where did I feel most aligned and fulfilled?
- What challenges or opportunities are calling me to expand further?
- What's one adjustment I can make to embody my Purpose fully?

Step 2: Refine and Sharpen Your Purpose Statement
Purpose evolves. Revisit and refine your Purpose Beyond the Self statement periodically to reflect your growth and new understanding. Keep it grounded in your unique gifts and values, and don't forget to deeply consider the impact you want to create.

STEP 3: BUILD YOUR LEGACY ONE LAYER AT A TIME
Ask yourself:

- What can I commit to this year that will deepen my contribution to the world?
- What skills, knowledge, or experiences will help me expand my capacity to contribute?
- Who can I partner with or learn from to magnify my impact?

So, What's the Point?
These exercises will help you integrate your Purpose Beyond

the Self into your life every time you practice them.

THE TOUGH TRUTHS

- You are far more capable than you could possibly realize.
- What you're really afraid of isn't failure, it's stepping into your own greatness.
- If you weren't meant to make an impact, you wouldn't feel this pull.
- Your comfort zone is nothing but a waiting room for regret.
- You already know what you need to do, the question is whether you'll do it.
- At the end of your life, there's only question that will matter: "Is the world a better place because I was in it?"

CLOSING WORDS

BEFORE WE FINISH, I want to say something simple but sincere: thank you for reading.

You now have everything you need. No missing pieces, no hidden secrets—just the truth about what it takes to live a life that actually matters.

At the very start of this book, I told you that most people don't change. Not because they can't, but because they don't take the leap. They get the insight, they feel the spark, and then they let it fade.

But a few won't.

A few will take what they've learned here and make it the foundation of a life they can truly feel proud of.

If that's you—if you're one of the few—then let's talk.

Scan the QR code to schedule a one-to-one conversation with me.

Whatever comes next is yours to create.

Make it meaningful.

—Max Stephens

What the F*ck Do You Actually Want?

APPENDIX

WELL DONE. YOU MADE IT.

But we're not done. Not yet.

Back in the introduction, we made a deal: **If you're willing to question everything you thought you knew, you'll leave with an answer.** Not just **interesting ideas**, but something **undeniable**.

This appendix is here to **close the loop**.

If you stop now, you'll walk away with theories. **If you keep going, you'll walk away with proof.**

Stay focused here.

HOW TO READ THE APPENDIX

One rule: Don't just take my word for it.

Yes, I've worked with some of the **highest-performing individuals on the planet**—Harvard grads, billion-dollar fund managers, Hollywood producers, professional athletes. **People at the absolute peak of their industries.**

And guess what?

They fall into the exact same traps.

The same **illusions**. The same **faulty thinking**. The same **patterns of dissatisfaction, even when they think they've already won.**

That's what sparked this book.

This appendix isn't here to **convince you**, it's here to **show you**. These are the studies that **shatter the myths you've been living** under. The research that **proves everything we've covered in this book isn't just theory, it's reality.**

And if there's one thing I don't want? **It's for you to accept these ideas just because they're in a fancy book by a very, very charismatic author.**

(That was a joke. In case you missed it.)

HOW THE APPENDIX WORKS

Each of the following sections will adhere to this format:

- **What the Study Reveals** → The core truth. No fluff. No jargon. Just **the brutal, undeniable insight.**
- **Where the World Gets It Wrong** → The **lies, misconceptions, and outdated narratives** that keep people stuck.
- **How to Test This in Your Own Life** → **Three direct challenges** to help you **see the proof in real time**—in your own experience.

That's it.

No extra commentary. No drawn-out explanations. **Just the evidence, the insight, and a way to see it for yourself.**

I'll prove it to you, let's begin.

APPENDIX TO CHAPTER 1
WHAT THE HELL IS GOING ON?

STUDY 1: THE TREADMILL EFFECT—WHY MORE NEVER FEELS LIKE ENOUGH

Brickman, P., & Campbell, D. T. (1971). *Hedonic adaptation: A theoretical and empirical exploration of the treadmill effect. Journal of Social and Clinical Psychology.*

What the Study Reveals:
Your brain is **rigged against you.** Brickman and Campbell introduced the concept of **hedonic adaptation,** proving that no matter what happens—whether you win the lottery, get a promotion, or buy your dream home—your happiness **will not last.** Your brain will **reset to baseline** and you'll start craving the next big thing. This isn't an accident. It's **biological programming.**

Where the World Gets It Wrong:
You've been **lied to.** Society sells you the idea that happiness is always **one achievement away.** But the moment you hit a milestone, the goalpost **moves.** That's why people with all the money, power, and luxury in the world still feel **empty inside.** They keep trying to win at a game that's designed to never end.

How to Test This in Your Own Life:
- **Call out your last big "win."** That promotion, that car, that relationship—how long did the high actually last before your brain started whispering, *Okay, what's next?* **Be brutally honest.**
- **Track your shifting goalposts.** Look at the **past version of you.** What did you once believe would finally make you happy? **Did it?** Or are you still chasing the same elusive finish line, just in a different form?
- **Catch the normalization effect.** The first time you stayed in a five-star hotel, flew business class, or got a raise, it felt **incredible.** Now? It's just **normal.** If every level-up eventually feels **boring,** then what's **actually** going to make you feel fulfilled?

STUDY 2: THE COMPARISON TRAP—WHY YOU'LL NEVER WIN THE GAME OF WHO'S DOING BETTER

Festinger, L. (1954). *A theory of social comparison processes. Human Relations.*

What the Study Reveals:
Your brain is **wired to make you miserable.** Festinger's **social comparison theory** proves that no matter how much you achieve, you will **always** find someone doing "better." Social media has made this a **nightmare**—you are now exposed to **thousands** of

people's curated highlight reels every day, and your brain isn't built to handle it.

Where the World Gets It Wrong:
You think competition drives success. **It doesn't.** Competition drives **misery**. Every time you compare yourself to someone else, you feel like you're losing—even when you're **winning**. That's why even millionaires feel like failures when they meet billionaires. The game is **rigged**.

How to Test This in Your Own Life:
- **Catch yourself in comparison mode.** Notice the last time you felt "behind." Was it because you **actually** wanted something, or because you saw someone else had it? **If social media didn't exist, would you still care?**
- **Observe how comparison hijacks your contentment.** Were you **happy** with your life until you saw someone else's? Pay attention to how **quickly** outside influences make you second-guess what actually matters to you.
- **Expose your unconscious competitors.** Who are you **silently measuring yourself against?** That person from college? Your more "successful" sibling? Someone you **don't even like**? Ask yourself **why the hell** they have so much power over your self-worth.

STUDY 3: MANUFACTURED DESIRE—WHY YOU WANT THINGS THAT WON'T MAKE YOU HAPPY

Baudrillard, J. (1970). *The consumer society: Myths and structures.* University of California Press.

What the Study Reveals:
You don't actually know what you want. **Companies do.** Baudrillard's research in consumer psychology proves that advertising doesn't just sell products—it **manufactures** desires. It **hijacks your brain** and rewires what you think will make you happy. Modern consumer culture shifts your goals from **meaning, purpose, and connection** to **status, possessions, and wealth**—so that you stay stuck in an endless loop of wanting **more**.

Where the World Gets It Wrong:
You've been **programmed** to believe that if you just buy the right things, you'll finally feel content. But the game is rigged. **If possessions actually satisfied you, companies would go out of business.** That's why trends change, why luxury brands sell exclusivity, and why the car that once made you feel powerful now just feels like **a car**. Those desires **aren't yours**—they were engineered.

How to Test This in Your Own Life:
- **Spot the corpse.** Think of something you **had to have**—a phone upgrade, a designer brand, the latest gadget. How

long did the thrill last before it became just another object in your life? **Did it actually change anything?**
- **Expose the illusion.** Do you really want that expensive watch, or do you want the **status** it signals? If no one else would see it, **would you still care?**
- **Destroy the marketing trap.** Next time you feel an urge to buy something, ask yourself: *Did I actually want this before I saw the ad?* If the answer is no, **you've just caught the machine manipulating you.**

STUDY 4: THE AMERICAN DREAM—WHY HARD WORK ALONE ISN'T ENOUGH

Chetty, R., et al. (2014). *Where is the land of opportunity? The geography of intergenerational mobility in the United States. Quarterly Journal of Economics.*

What the Study Reveals:
The idea that **hard work guarantees success** is a **fairy tale.** Chetty's research on **economic mobility** analyzed decades of data and found that **where you're born** determines your financial success **more than how hard you work.** The rich get richer not because they work harder, but because they have **better schools, stronger networks, and built-in financial safety nets.** Hard work **matters**, but effort without opportunity is like **trying to run a marathon with weights strapped to your ankles.**

Where the World Gets It Wrong:
The world worships **self-made success stories**, but conveniently ignores the **invisible advantages** behind them. The idea that **anyone can succeed if they just work hard enough** is a **lie**—one that keeps people **blaming themselves** instead of questioning the system. If success was really just about effort, janitors working three jobs would be billionaires.

How to Test This in Your Own Life:
- **Audit your starting line.** What advantages (or disadvantages) did you **inherit?** Were there **networks, resources, or safety nets** that helped you get ahead? Or obstacles that made things harder?
- **Pull back the curtain.** Think about someone you admire for their success. **Did they really do it alone?** Or were there mentors, financial safety nets, and lucky breaks they **never** talk about?
- **Challenge your programming.** Have you ever judged yourself—or others—for struggling, assuming it was just about **not working hard enough?** Who benefits from you believing that?

STUDY 5: THE DIGITAL AGE AND THE DECLINE OF DEEP CONNECTION

Turkle, S. (2015). *Reclaiming conversation: The power of talk in a digital age. Penguin Press.*

What the Study Reveals:
You are **lonelier than ever**, despite being more connected than ever. Turkle's research on **digital communication** proves that while social media and texting have **increased** the number of interactions, they've **weakened** their depth. Digital conversations **lack emotional nuance**, leaving people feeling **isolated and unseen**. Scrolling through updates isn't **connecting**—it's watching life through a glass screen.

Where the World Gets It Wrong:
We act like technology has made relationships **stronger. It hasn't.** A hundred Instagram likes don't replace a real conversation. A million text exchanges don't replace **face-to-face connection.** We mistake **interaction for intimacy,** and that's why so many people feel **alone, even with thousands of "friends."**

How to Test This in Your Own Life:
- **Audit your last "deep" conversation.** When was the last time you had an **actual, uninterrupted, meaningful conversation**—without a screen involved? **Be honest.**
- **Measure your post-social media mood.** After scrolling for 30 minutes, do you feel **more connected** or like you're **on the outside looking in?** If it's the latter, what does that tell you?

- **Expose your digital habits.** Are you **actually present** with people, or are you **half-distracted** by notifications? If your closest relationships feel **shallow, fix it** before it's too late.

APPENDIX TO CHAPTER 2
HOW DO I GET OUT?

STUDY 6: NARRATIVE PSYCHOLOGY—HOW THE STORIES YOU TELL YOURSELF CONTROL YOUR LIFE

McAdams, D. P. (1993). *The stories we live by: Personal myths and the making of the self. Guilford Press.*

What the Study Reveals:
Your life isn't defined by what happens to you—it's defined by **the story you tell yourself** about what happens to you. McAdams's research in **narrative psychology** proves that we don't just experience life; we **interpret it through a script** that we've been unconsciously writing since childhood. And here's the kicker: Most people are **running on scripts they didn't even write.**

Where the World Gets It Wrong:
You think you're **an independent thinker**, making your own decisions. But **you're not**—not unless you've actively rewritten the story you've been handed. Your beliefs about success, happiness, and purpose? **Inherited.** If you grew up somewhere else, you'd have an entirely different script. **You're not living your life— you're playing a role you were cast in.**

How to Test This in Your Own Life:
- **Interrogate your origin story.** What's the narrative you've been telling yourself about who you are? Are you the "hard worker," the "underdog," the "perfectionist"? **Who gave you that role?**
- **Expose the outside influences.** Were your goals, values, and dreams actually chosen by you—or were they handed to you by parents, teachers, or society? **Would you still want them if you grew up in a different country?**
- **Rewrite the script.** If **no one was watching**, if you had nothing to prove—what would you actually do with your life? That answer is what's real.

STUDY 7: THE CONSUMER IDENTITY CRISIS—HOW YOUR STUFF HIJACKS YOUR SENSE OF SELF

Belk, R. W. (1988). *Possessions and the extended self.* **Journal of Consumer Research.**

What the Study Reveals:
You don't just **own things**—you attach your **identity** to them. Belk's research shows that people use possessions to **tell their story**—which is why buying something **feels** like it changes who you are, even though it doesn't. This is why luxury brands are so powerful. A Rolex isn't just a watch, it's **a symbol**. A Porsche isn't just a car, it's a **statement**. But here's the problem: If your identity is built on **things**, who are you without them?

Where the World Gets It Wrong:
We act like buying something **changes us**. But it doesn't—it just **adds to the illusion**. A new wardrobe, a flashy car, a bigger house—it **feels** like an upgrade to your identity, but in reality, **it's just a temporary hit of dopamine**. The moment society stops valuing that thing, so do you. **You never wanted the object—you wanted the status it gave you.**

How to Test This in Your Own Life:
- **Find the corpse of an old obsession.** What's something you **had to have** a few years ago that now feels completely unimportant? If it really mattered, why doesn't it anymore?
- **Call out the status games.** Do you actually love luxury items, or do you love **what they make you look like?** If no one would ever see it, **would you still want it?**
- **Test your identity without your stuff.** If you lost everything—your car, your designer clothes, your latest gadgets—who would you be? If that question makes you uncomfortable, **you've built your self-worth on sand.**

STUDY 8: THE DEFAULT LIFE—HOW SOCIETY PRE-WROTE YOUR LIFE PLAN WITHOUT YOUR CONSENT

Iyengar, S. (2010). *The art of choosing.* **Hachette Books.**

What the Study Reveals:
Most people **aren't making choices**—they're just **following the pre-set path**. Iyengar's research on **choice architecture** reveals that human beings rarely start from scratch. Instead, we take whatever's given to us—whatever's **easiest, most acceptable, and most expected**—and call it a decision. The result? Most people **sleepwalk through life**, assuming they're in control, when really, they're just following **the default settings**.

Where the World Gets It Wrong:
We tell ourselves we're **in charge of our destiny**. But be honest: **Did you actively choose your career, your beliefs, your lifestyle—or did they just ... happen?** Society pushes you toward **the default template**: school, degree, job, marriage, mortgage, retirement. Did you ever stop and ask yourself if that's what you actually wanted? **Or did you just assume it was the only option?**

How to Test This in Your Own Life:
- **Interrogate your biggest life choices.** Did you choose your career, or did you just follow what made the most sense at the time? What about your relationships? Your lifestyle? If you weren't expected to follow a certain path, **what would you be doing differently?**

- **Catch the "that's just the way it is" excuse.** If you feel stuck, is it because the situation is truly inescapable, or because you **never considered alternatives?**
- **Imagine a blank slate.** If you woke up tomorrow with **no obligations, no expectations, no pressure—what kind of life would you build from scratch?** If that answer doesn't match the life you have now, **what the hell are you waiting for?**

STUDY 9: PSYCHOLOGICAL GROWTH—WHY STAYING THE SAME IS SLOWLY KILLING YOU

Kegan, R. (1994). *In over our heads: The mental demands of modern life.* Harvard University Press.

What the Study Reveals:
You are **not meant to stay the same person forever.** Kegan's research on **adult development** proves that humans are designed to evolve past **cultural conditioning**, break old mental frameworks, and create their **own** understanding of life. But here's the uncomfortable truth: **Most people don't make it that far.** They stay stuck at the same mental level they were in their early twenties, clinging to outdated beliefs that were **handed to them** instead of developed through actual thinking.

Where the World Gets It Wrong:
We reward **conformity**, not evolution. If you question the status quo, you'll make people uncomfortable. If you **outgrow** the people around you, they'll tell you you're "changing too

much." **But isn't that the point?** If you haven't significantly changed your world-view in the last **five years**, that's not stability—it's **stagnation**.

How to Test This in Your Own Life:
- **Check for outdated beliefs.** What's something you strongly believed ten years ago that now seems ridiculous? If nothing comes to mind, **you haven't evolved.**
- **Look at the people around you.** Are they **growing**, challenging their perspectives, evolving? Or are they just repeating the same cycles over and over? If it's the latter, **you might be stuck in the same loop.**
- **Ask yourself: Who benefits from your stagnation?** Growth is disruptive. It challenges the system. If you've never felt outside resistance for changing your mind, you're probably not **changing enough.**

STUDY 10: THE MORE-MATERIALISM MYTH—WHY CHASING WEALTH WON'T MAKE YOU HAPPY

Kasser, T., & Ryan, R. M. (1996). *A dark side of the American dream: Correlates of financial success as a central life aspiration. Journal of Personality and Social Psychology.*

What the Study Reveals:
More **does not** equal better. Kasser and Ryan's research on **materialism and life satisfaction** found that people who focus on

wealth, status, and material success are significantly **less happy** than those who prioritize **growth, relationships, and meaning.** The more you chase **external validation,** the emptier you feel inside.

Where the World Gets It Wrong:
Society sells the dream that **if you just get rich enough, you'll finally be happy.** But why, then, are so many of the world's most "successful" people depressed, lost, and empty? Because wealth is a **terrible substitute** for purpose. If money truly solved the problem, billionaires would be **the most fulfilled people on the planet**—and they're not.

How to Test This in Your Own Life:
- **Ask yourself what's actually making you happy.** Is it what you own, or is it the experiences, relationships, and meaning behind those things?
- **Look at the people you admire.** Are they rich and hollow, or do they have something **deeper** anchoring them?
- **Consider this: If your net worth doubled overnight, would your life suddenly have meaning?** Think deeply on this.

APPENDIX TO CHAPTER 3
WHAT DO I DO FIRST?

STUDY 11: RADICAL HONESTY—HOW LYING SLOWLY DESTROYS YOU

Blanton, B. (1994). *Radical honesty: How to transform your life by telling the truth.* TarcherPerigee.

What the Study Reveals:
Every time you lie, even in small ways, you **chip away at yourself.** Blanton's research proves that dishonesty doesn't just deceive others—it **erodes your own sense of self.** The more you censor, filter, or manipulate the truth, the further you drift from who you actually are. You start living as a **performance,** and before long, even you can't tell where the act ends and the real you begins. Radical honesty isn't just about telling the truth—it's about **escaping the bullshit version of yourself you've created to fit in.**

Where the World Gets It Wrong:
Society **runs on lies.** You're expected to fake enthusiasm in job interviews, soften your opinions to avoid "offending" people, and curate a **false version of yourself** for social media. The world doesn't want your truth—it wants you **polished and palatable.** But here's the cost: Every lie, no matter how small, **locks you**

deeper into a fake life. You wake up one day **trapped in a personality you built for others** instead of living as yourself.

How to Test This in Your Own Life:
- **Pay attention to your everyday lies.** How often do you soften the truth to keep the peace? **How much of your life is performative?**
- **Say what you actually think—just once.** Pick a moment today to **stop filtering.** See how uncomfortable it feels. That discomfort? **That's proof of how conditioned you are to lie.**
- **Ask yourself: Would the people in your life still like you if they knew the unfiltered version of you?** If not, are they even your people?

STUDY 12: THE PRISON OF RESENTMENT— WHY HOLDING A GRUDGE IS RUINING YOUR LIFE

Worthington, E. L. Jr. (2001). *Forgiveness and reconciliation: Theory and applications.* Springer Publishing.

What the Study Reveals:
Holding onto resentment doesn't **punish** the other person—it **poisons you.** Worthington's research proves that **grudges wreck your mental and physical health,** spiking stress hormones, weakening your immune system, and keeping your brain locked in a loop of anger. Forgiveness isn't about letting someone off the

hook—it's about **freeing yourself from the mental real estate that resentment occupies.**

Where the World Gets It Wrong:
We glorify **holding grudges** as if resentment is some kind of **moral high ground.** The world teaches you that **forgiveness is weak**—that if you let go, you're giving up your power. But that's backwards: **Holding onto resentment doesn't give you control—it hands control over to the person you hate.** You're not making them suffer—you're **carrying their bullshit for no good reason.**

How to Test This in Your Own Life:
- **Think of someone who wronged you.** Now, be honest—do they even think about you? Or are you the only one still carrying this weight?
- **Catch yourself replaying old wounds.** How much mental space does your resentment take up? **Imagine if you used that energy for something that actually benefited you.**
- **Ask yourself: If I knew I had six months to live, would this grudge still be worth my time?** If the answer is no, **why are you wasting your life on it now?**

STUDY 13: THE ENERGY DRAIN OF HOLDING GRUDGES

Witvliet, C. O. (2001). *Forgiveness and health: An exploratory study of the effects of forgiveness on health-related outcomes. Journal of Social and Clinical Psychology.*

What the Study Reveals:
Resentment isn't just an **emotion**—it's an **energy vampire**. Witvliet's research proves that replaying past wrongs makes you **mentally exhausted and physically depleted** as well. People who refuse to forgive show **higher cortisol levels, increased anxiety, and worse problem-solving skills**. Every moment spent **dwelling on old wounds** is a moment stolen from **building your future**.

Where the World Gets It Wrong:
Society pushes the **revenge fantasy**—the idea that **holding onto anger makes you strong**. But **true strength isn't about holding on— it's about letting go**. The energy you're wasting **replaying old betrayals** and hanging on to **resentment and retribution** is energy you could be using to **build something better**. **You're not punishing them—you're punishing yourself.**

How to Test This in Your Own Life:
- **Calculate the cost of your grudges.** How much mental space do they take up? How often do you **catch yourself replaying old fights or thinking about people you "hate"**?
- **Flip the perspective.** Imagine someone is **still obsessing over**

something you did years ago. Would you care? That's exactly how much the people you hate think about you.
- Ask yourself: What would happen if I stopped carrying this? If you suddenly had **all that energy back**, what would you do with it?

STUDY 14: MORTALITY—THE TRUTH YOU KEEP RUNNING FROM

Solomon, S., Greenberg, J., & Pyszczynski, T. (1986). *The psychology of terror. Scientific American.*

What the Study Reveals:
The moment you **accept your own mortality**, everything changes. Solomon's research shows that people who **face the reality of death head-on** stop wasting time on **bullshit**. They **cut distractions, drop meaningless goals, and prioritize what actually matters.** But most people **live in denial**—pretending they have all the time in the world, putting off everything important until **it's too late.**

Where the World Gets It Wrong:
We act like **thinking about death is morbid**—but ignoring it is what's truly insane. Death is **the only certainty in life**, yet you're encouraged to **live as if you're immortal.** You waste time, stay in situations that drain you, and **put off living until "later."** But **later is never guaranteed.** If you're not **facing the fact that you're going to die**, you're **not really living at all.**

How to Test This in Your Own Life:
- **Imagine your own funeral.** What would people say about you right now? More importantly, **is it what you would actually want them to say?**
- **Audit your life choices.** If **you knew** you only had a year left, what would you change? **Why aren't you changing it now?**
- **Sit with the fact that you will die.** Not as an abstract idea— **really feel it.** What suddenly seems urgent? What suddenly seems like a waste of time?

STUDY 15: THE HIDDEN FEAR THAT CONTROLS YOUR LIFE

Becker, E. (1973). *The denial of death. Free Press.*

What the Study Reveals:
Every decision you make is **subconsciously shaped by your fear of death.** Becker's research proves that people **distract themselves with work, status, and material success** not because they **truly care about those things,** but because they're **desperate to ignore their own mortality.** When you finally **stop running from death,** you stop **wasting your life chasing bullshit.**

Where the World Gets It Wrong:
People think they're chasing success, validation, and security— but **they're really chasing immortality.** That's why billionaires hoard wealth they'll never spend, why people cling to legacies, why you **grind for status you don't even enjoy.** You're **terrified of**

being forgotten, so you throw yourself into **any distraction that keeps you from facing the truth: You will die, and none of this will matter unless you make it matter.**

How to Test This in Your Own Life:
- **Examine what you're chasing.** Is your ambition about **creating something meaningful,** or is it just **a way to outrun your own fear of insignificance?**
- **Strip away the external rewards.** If no one would **ever know** about your achievements, would you still want them?
- **Face the inevitable.** If you died tomorrow, what in your life would have been **pointless?** What would have actually mattered? **Start living accordingly.**

APPENDIX TO CHAPTER 4
WHY DO I EVEN NEED A PURPOSE BEYOND THE SELF?

STUDY 16: EVOLUTION DIDN'T MAKE YOU SELFISH—CULTURE DID

Wilson, D. S. (1998). *Evolution for everyone: How Darwin's theory can change the way we think about our lives. Delta.*

What the Study Reveals:
The idea that **self-interest leads to success is a complete lie.** Wilson's research in evolutionary psychology proves that humans **survived and thrived not because of ruthless competition, but because of cooperation and contribution.** Altruism isn't some noble, feel-good concept—it's the reason **you exist today.** The strongest societies weren't built on individualism; they were built by people who **looked out for each other.** The truth? **You're biologically wired to contribute—not to go it alone.**

Where the World Gets It Wrong:
The "self-made" myth is **one of the greatest scams of modern culture.** Hustle culture and hyper-individualism convince you that **if you're not doing everything alone, you're weak.** But Wilson's research shows that **selfishness might win short-term battles, but cooperation wins wars.** The most successful, adaptive, and

powerful communities are built on shared responsibility, not individual achievement.

How to Test This in Your Own Life:
- **List the people who have helped you get where you are.** Do you actually believe you got here alone? Or are you just **refusing to acknowledge your debts?**
- **Think about your biggest achievements.** Were they **truly solo victories,** or were they built on the **support, knowledge, and efforts of others?**
- Ask yourself: Would I be further ahead if I stopped seeing dependence as weakness and started seeing contribution as power?

STUDY 17: PURPOSE ISN'T A LUXURY—IT'S SURVIVAL

Buettner, D. (2008). *The blue zones: Lessons for living longer from the people who've lived the longest. National Geographic Society.*

What the Study Reveals:
The longest-living people on Earth don't just **eat well and exercise**—they have **a reason to wake up in the morning.** Buettner's research on **Blue Zones,** regions where people routinely live past 100, proves that **having a clear purpose isn't just psychologically beneficial—it literally extends your life.** The Japanese call it *ikigai,* meaning "a reason for being." People who stay engaged,

contribute, and **have something meaningful to do** live longer, healthier, and happier lives.

Where the World Gets It Wrong:
You've been **lied to about retirement.** The idea that you should **work yourself into the ground, then finally relax at the end** is complete **bullshit.** The happiest, healthiest people don't "check out" once they hit a certain age—they **stay engaged.** Purpose isn't optional. **It's biological.** Waiting until later to find meaning isn't just a waste of time—it's a direct path to **burnout, depression, and an early grave.**

How to Test This in Your Own Life:
- **Look at the happiest people in your life.** Are they the ones who **live for weekends** or the ones who have a deep sense of purpose?
- **Ask yourself: What's something I do that makes time disappear?** That's a clue to what actually matters to you.
- **Imagine waking up tomorrow with no responsibilities.** Nothing to build. Nothing to contribute to. **Would you actually be happy—or just lost?**

STUDY 18: WHY AVOIDING WORK IS MAKING YOU MISERABLE

Csikszentmihalyi, M. (1990). *Flow: The psychology of optimal experience. Harper & Row.*

What the Study Reveals:
Csikszentmihalyi's research on **flow** proves that people are happiest when they're **fully immersed in something meaningful.** True fulfillment doesn't come from **escaping work**—it comes from being so engaged in what you're doing that you **lose track of time.** And the key factor? **The challenge must matter.** People thrive when they contribute in a way that stretches their abilities and serves something **bigger than themselves.**

Where the World Gets It Wrong:
Modern culture teaches you that happiness comes from **avoiding work**—from binge-watching Netflix, taking vacations, and minimizing effort. But Csikszentmihalyi's research proves that's **complete garbage. Checking out makes you restless.** Engaging deeply makes you **alive.** The real question isn't *"How do I do less work?"* It's *"How do I make my work meaningful?"*

How to Test This in Your Own Life:
- **Think about the last time you were so focused you forgot to check the time.** What were you doing, and why was it so engaging?
- **Look at how often you feel restless.** If you're constantly bored, ask yourself: **Are you actually overworked, or are you just doing**

meaningless shit?

- Ask yourself: What if I stopped trying to escape work and instead built a life around work that actually mattered to me?

STUDY 19: CONTRIBUTION IS THE CHEAT CODE FOR HAPPINESS

Batson, C. D. (1991). *The altruism question: Toward a social-psychological answer.* **Lawrence Erlbaum Associates.**

What the Study Reveals:
Helping others isn't **just** good for them—it's **biochemically good for you.** Batson's research proves that **acts of kindness and generosity** trigger dopamine and serotonin pathways in your brain, leading to **reduced stress, greater happiness, and even better physical health.** Helping others isn't **a sacrifice**—it's a **neuroscientific life hack** for feeling better.

Where the World Gets It Wrong:
Society treats **contribution as an afterthought**—something you do **once you've taken care of yourself.** But Batson's research **flips that idea upside down:** Helping others **is the most selfish thing you can do** because it directly improves your own well-being. The idea that you have to **choose between helping yourself and helping others** is a lie. **They're the same thing.**

How to Test This in Your Own Life:
- Think about the last time you did something for someone else. Did it drain you, or did it make you feel better?
- Look at the people who seem genuinely happy. Are they the ones obsessed with **hoarding success**, or the ones actively **giving to others**?
- Ask yourself: If I measured my success by what I gave instead of what I got, how would my priorities shift?

STUDY 20: WHY CHASING STATUS WILL NEVER SATISFY YOU

Deci, E. L., & Ryan, R. M. (2000). *The "what" and "why" of goal pursuits: Human needs and the self-determination of behavior. Psychological Inquiry.*

What the Study Reveals:
Deci and Ryan's **Self-Determination Theory** exposes the brutal truth about motivation: **Extrinsic rewards (money, status, fame) don't actually fulfill you.** Their research proves that people who chase external validation experience **higher levels of anxiety, dissatisfaction, and burnout.** Meanwhile, those who pursue **intrinsic goals (growth, relationships, and contribution)** report **higher long-term well-being and deeper fulfillment.**

Where the World Gets It Wrong:
Society convinces you that **if you grind hard enough, happiness will come later.** That **once you hit the right milestone,** you'll finally

feel complete. But Deci and Ryan's research proves that's **a trap**—because the journey itself determines the outcome. If you **hate your process**, you'll **hate your result**. Chasing **external validation without meaning** just leaves you burned out at the finish line, wondering **why the prize feels hollow.**

How to Test This in Your Own Life:
- **Think about something you worked insanely hard for.** Did the reward actually feel as good as you expected, or was the process itself more meaningful?
- **Audit how much of your time is spent chasing validation.** Are your goals truly **yours,** or are they **shaped by what looks impressive to others?**
- **Ask yourself: If no one would ever see or know about my future achievements, would I still want them?** If the answer is no, **you're chasing a borrowed dream.**

APPENDIX TO CHAPTER 5
WHAT'S IN IT FOR ME?

STUDY 21: PURPOSE IS THE ULTIMATE SURVIVAL MECHANISM

Frankl, V. E. (1946). *Man's search for meaning.* **Beacon Press.**

What the Study Reveals:
Frankl's story, based on his experience surviving **Auschwitz**, proved that **meaning is the key to psychological resilience.** His story shows that people who anchor themselves to a purpose beyond their own survival don't just endure suffering—they **transform it.** Purpose is more than a feel-good concept; it's **the difference between those who break and those who overcome.**

Where the World Gets It Wrong:
Modern culture worships **comfort and convenience,** selling you the idea that **happiness comes from eliminating struggle.** But Frankl's research **obliterates that myth:** A meaningful life isn't free of suffering—it just makes suffering **worth something.** The strongest, most fulfilled people aren't the ones who avoided pain; they're the ones who **used it to build something greater than themselves.**

How to Test This in Your Own Life:
- **Think about the hardest moment in your life.** What actually got you through it—temporary distractions or something bigger than yourself?
- **Look at the people who inspire you most.** Are they the ones who **played it safe**, or the ones who fought for something beyond their own comfort?
- **Ask yourself: What if I stopped running from discomfort and started using it to fuel something meaningful?**

STUDY 22: YOUR BRAIN IS HARDWIRED FOR PURPOSE, NOT CHEAP DOPAMINE HITS

Davidson, R. J. (2012). *The emotional life of your brain: How its unique patterns affect the way you think, feel, and live—and how you can change them.* Penguin.

What the Study Reveals:
Davidson's research proves that **people with a sense of purpose experience a longer-lasting release of dopamine** than those who chase material success or short-term pleasure. Unlike **the fleeting highs of consumerism, entertainment, or social validation,** engaging in meaningful work literally **rewires your brain for sustained well-being.** If you feel like **nothing is ever enough,** it's not because you don't have enough pleasure—it's because you don't have enough **purpose.**

Where the World Gets It Wrong:
Society tells you happiness comes from **consumption**—buying shit, watching Netflix, upgrading your life. But **pleasure is weak fuel.** Davidson's research proves that **real happiness isn't a fleeting high—it's a neurological state built through meaning.** If you constantly need **new stimulation to feel satisfied, the problem isn't that you need something more—it's that you need something deeper.**

How to Test This in Your Own Life:
- **Notice how quickly the high from buying something fades.** Is it actually making you fulfilled, or just distracting you?
- **Think about the most meaningful moment of your life.** Was it about what you consumed, or about what you created, contributed, or built?
- **Ask yourself: If I started prioritizing long-term meaning over short-term pleasure, how would my choices change?**

STUDY 23: WHY SOME PEOPLE LOVE THEIR WORK (AND OTHERS HATE THEIRS)

Wrzesniewski, A. (2003). *Finding meaning in work. In E. A. Locke (Ed.), Handbook of work satisfaction. Lexington Books.*

What the Study Reveals:
Wrzesniewski's research **shatters the idea that career satisfaction comes from the job itself.** People in **the exact same profession** (janitors, doctors, CEOs) experience vastly different levels

of happiness depending on whether they see their work as a calling or just a paycheck. The happiest people don't wait for meaning to find them—they actively create it by seeing their work as part of a greater whole.

Where the World Gets It Wrong:
You've been told to prioritize financial security first and chase meaning later—but Wrzesniewski's research proves that's backwards thinking. Fulfillment isn't reserved for the rich or lucky; it's a choice. If your work feels meaningless now, more money won't fix that. The happiest people don't search for purpose later—they build it into what they do right now.

How to Test This in Your Own Life:
- **Look at your current job.** Do you see it as just a way to make money, or as something that contributes to a bigger picture?
- **Think about the happiest people you know.** Do they just clock in for a paycheck, or do they see their work as part of something important?
- **Ask yourself: If I had all the money I ever needed, what kind of work would I still want to do?**

STUDY 24: GIVING IS THE SHORTCUT TO HAPPINESS

Luks, A. (1991). *Helping and happiness: The effect of helping on happiness in a natural setting. Journal of Social Psychology.*

What the Study Reveals:
Luks's research introduced the term **"Helper's High"** after proving that **giving triggers a physiological reward system in the brain.** Acts of generosity—whether through mentoring, volunteering, or simply helping someone—cause **a surge of endorphins, lower stress, and even strengthen the immune system.** Helping others doesn't **deplete** you—it literally **makes you feel better.**

Where the World Gets It Wrong:
Society conditions you to believe that **giving is a sacrifice**—that generosity drains you, and that you need to **secure your own success before you can contribute.** But Luks's research **proves the opposite:** Giving isn't something you do **once you're happy and successful**—it's **the path to becoming happy and successful.** The irony? **The people who focus only on their own happiness are usually the most miserable.**

How to Test This in Your Own Life:
- **Think of the last time you truly helped someone.** Did it exhaust you, or did it leave you feeling more energized?
- **Notice your mental state when you focus on yourself versus when you contribute.** Which mindset actually makes you

feel more alive?
- Ask yourself: If I started seeing contribution as fuel instead of sacrifice, how would I approach my life differently?

STUDY 25: YOUR LEGACY IS THE ONLY THING THAT WILL MATTER IN THE END

Carstensen, L. L. (2011). *Aging and the social world: A lifespan perspective.* **Stanford University Press.**

What the Study Reveals:
Carstensen's research on **lifespan psychology** found that as people age, their priorities shift toward **legacy**—what they leave behind, how they're remembered, and whether their life actually mattered. Her findings show that people who engage in meaningful contributions, whether through mentorship, creative work, or service, report **higher satisfaction, lower anxiety, and greater peace of mind.** Simply put: **You need to matter to more than just yourself.**

Where the World Gets It Wrong:
We treat **success as the end goal**—make money, get titles, reach the top. But Carstensen's research **destroys that idea: Success without significance is meaningless.** The people who look back on their lives with regret aren't the ones who **failed to make money**—they're the ones who failed to **make a difference.** The real metric of a life well-lived isn't **what you had, but what you gave.**

How to Test This in Your Own Life:
- **Imagine yourself at 80, looking back on your life.** What will actually matter?
- **Think about someone whose legacy impacted you.** Was it their wealth and status, or what they **contributed to the world?**
- **Ask yourself: If I disappeared tomorrow, would the world feel my absence—or would it move on without noticing?**

APPENDIX TO CHAPTER 6
CALLING ME A HERO IS A BIT MUCH, ISN'T IT?

STUDY 26: YOU'RE MORE POWERFUL THAN YOU THINK—HOW SMALL ACTS CREATE MASSIVE CHANGE

Christakis, N. A., & Fowler, J. H. (2010). *Connected: The surprising power of our social networks and how they shape our lives.* Back Bay Books.

What the Study Reveals:
Your impact extends **way beyond what you see.** Christakis and Fowler's research proves that kindness spreads in social networks **up to three degrees of separation.** That means **every action you take ripples through your environment**—affecting not just the person in front of you, but how they treat others, and how *those* people treat even more people.

Where the World Gets It Wrong:
We tell ourselves **one person can't change anything**—that the world is too big, too broken, too chaotic. **Bullshit.** This study proves that even **the smallest action** can trigger **massive consequences.** Your choices are **contagious.** The only question is—what kind of effect are you actually having?

How to Test This in Your Own Life:
- Think about a time someone's kindness shifted your whole mood. Did they even know the impact they had on you?
- Watch how your attitude affects the people around you. Do you bring people up, or drag them down without realizing it?
- Ask yourself: If every action I take is shaping the world around me, am I creating a chain reaction I'd actually be proud of?

STUDY 27: HEROISM IS A CHOICE, NOT A BIRTHRIGHT

Zimbardo, P. (2008). *The Lucifer effect: Understanding how good people turn evil. Random House.*

What the Study Reveals:
Zimbardo's research **destroys the myth** that heroes are born different. His findings prove that **anyone** can rise to the occasion when they choose to **step up** in critical moments. Courage **isn't about fearlessness—it's about acting despite fear.** The difference between a bystander and a hero? **A single decision.**

Where the World Gets It Wrong:
Society loves to glorify **"exceptional people"**—as if heroism is reserved for a special few. **Wrong.** The reality? Most people hesitate, waiting for someone else to take the lead. **Heroes aren't different from you—they just stopped waiting.**

How to Test This in Your Own Life:
- Think about a moment when you hesitated to speak up or act. What stopped you?
- Remember a time when you stepped up, even in a small way. What made you do it?
- Ask yourself: If heroism is just the choice to act, what's stopping me from being the person who steps up?

STUDY 28: PURPOSE IS THE ULTIMATE CHEAT CODE FOR GRIT

Duckworth, A. (2016). *Grit: The power of passion and perseverance. Scribner.*

What the Study Reveals:
Duckworth's research proves that **grit—the ability to push through challenges—comes from having a deeper purpose.** People who connect their struggles to **something bigger than themselves** recover faster, persist longer, and refuse to quit when others do. **Purpose fuels resilience**—without it, you're just forcing yourself through misery.

Where the World Gets It Wrong:
You've been told that **resilience is about toughness**—grinding through adversity with sheer willpower. **Nope.** The truth? **Grit isn't about forcing yourself to suffer—it's about knowing why the hell you're fighting in the first place.** The stronger your purpose, the less you even consider giving up.

How to Test This in Your Own Life:
- **Think about a time you stuck with something difficult.** What made you keep going?
- **Look at something you gave up on.** Was it because you lacked ability—or because it didn't feel meaningful enough?
- **Ask yourself: If my current struggles were part of something bigger, how would that change the way I approach them?**

STUDY 29: YOUR SELF-IMAGE IS THE CEILING OF YOUR POTENTIAL

Dweck, C. S. (2013). *Mindset: The new psychology of success. Ballantine Books.*

What the Study Reveals:
Dweck's research on **growth mindset** proves that the way you see yourself **literally determines how you act.** People who believe they can grow, improve, and contribute **take action.** Those who believe they're powerless? **They stay on the sidelines.** The moment you see yourself as someone who matters, **you start behaving like it.**

Where the World Gets It Wrong:
Most people wait for **external validation** before believing they're capable of making a difference. **That's backwards.** The truth? **You don't act because you believe—you believe because you act.** The moment you start **playing bigger,** your self-image will catch up.

How to Test This in Your Own Life:
- **Notice the stories you tell yourself about your abilities.** Do they empower you or hold you back?
- **Think about a time you proved yourself wrong.** What did you believe you couldn't do—until you did it?
- **Ask yourself: If I fully believed I could change the world in some way, how would I start showing up differently?**

STUDY 30: YOU'RE ALREADY ON YOUR HERO'S JOURNEY—WHETHER YOU REALIZE IT OR NOT

Campbell, J. (1949). *The hero with a thousand faces.* **Princeton University Press.**

What the Study Reveals:
Campbell's research uncovered **a universal blueprint for transformation**—the **Hero's Journey**. Across **every culture and era**, stories of growth follow the same pattern: **You're called to something bigger. You face trials. You struggle. You transform.** This isn't just fiction—it's how humans evolve.

Where the World Gets It Wrong:
People think **heroic stories** are for legends, movies, or other people. But Campbell's research proves that **this pattern applies to you, right now.** Your struggles, setbacks, and challenges? They're not random—they're part of your transformation. You

are already on your **Hero's Journey**—whether you accept the call or not.

How to Test This in Your Own Life:
- **Think about a major struggle you've faced.** What did it force you to learn?
- **Look at the moments that changed you.** Can you see how they shaped you into someone stronger?
- **Ask yourself:** If I stopped resisting my own evolution and embraced the journey, what would happen next?

ABOUT THE AUTHOR

Max Stephens isn't your coach. He's what comes after your coach stops working.

He doesn't believe your problem is a lack of clarity, confidence, discipline, or morning routines. He's not here to help you *optimize your calendar* or *believe in yourself*. He's here to ask the question none of those "positive mindset" peddlers want you to confront:

What the fuck do you really want?

Max works with high performers who've ticked every box society told them to, and are quietly panicking that they still feel empty. He calls bullshit on the cult of productivity, the lie of "success equals fulfillment," and the myth that you can fix your existential dread with breathwork and a green juice.

He's a personal development strategist who helps ambitious people stop playing the game they never actually chose, and start building a life that matters. His approach is raw, rigorous, and rooted in developmental theory, ontological coaching, effective conversational practice, and a very healthy disrespect for cultural conditioning.

This book is not here to inspire you.

It's here to break the trance.

If you make it to the end, you'll know where to find him.

maxstephenscoaching.com

www.ingramcontent.com/pod-product-compliance
Lightning Source LLC
Chambersburg PA
CBHW031248290426
44109CB00012B/487